Heroes, Villains & Victims

·OF NORWICH·

Heroes, Villains & Victims

·OF NORWICH·

Pamela Brooks

breedon **books**
PUBLISHING

First published in Great Britain in 2008 by
The Breedon Books Publishing Company Limited
Breedon House, 3 The Parker Centre,
Derby, DE21 4SZ.

ISBN: 978-1-85983-627-9

Printed and bound by Cromwell Press Ltd., Trowbridge, Wiltshire.

Contents

For Gerard, Christopher and Chloë, with all my love.

Preface

Norwich has seen so many characters – heroes, villains and victims – that I could have written a whole shelf on the subject; the hardest part of writing this book was choosing who to keep in and who to leave out. So much has already been written about Kett and Rush; but in a book about Norwich's heroes, villains and victims, how could I leave out Norwich's most high-profile rebel and Norfolk's most notorious murderer? Ditto Edith Cavell, our best-known war heroine, and Elizabeth Fry, the prison reformer who grew up in our city: they're both deservedly well known but I still felt their stories ought to be included here.

I hope you'll also discover tales of people new to you – tales of people who made a difference, both to Norwich and to the wider community. People who were heroes, villains, victims – and sometimes all three because, in Norwich, we 'do different'. There are one or two tales here that will make uncomfortable reading – but I would like to think that in modern times our community would have reacted to the circumstances in a very different way.

This is also the place where I would like to say thank you. First of all to my husband Gerard and my children Christopher and Chloë, for giving me time in the library and record office and for letting me hijack family outings to take photographs. To Dot Lumley, my agent, as always, for her support and encouragement. To Michelle Grainger and Steve Caron at Breedon, for giving me the chance to tell these stories. To my fellow historian Neil Storey, for reminding me about Dorothy Jewson. And, last but not least, very grateful thanks to the people who loaned me photographs or allowed me to take photographs of items in their care: the Hospital Art Project (which looks after the historic collections of the Norwich and Norwich Hospital University Trust), Norfolk County Library and Information Services (particularly to Clare Agate, Maxine Block and the staff at the Heritage Centre), Helen Renton from Strangers' Hall Museum, Norma Watt from the Castle Museum, Julie Bunn from Barrett & Coe, the University of East Anglia, the Church of St Peter Mancroft, Chawton House Library and the Norfolk and Norwich Association for the Blind.

Pamela Brooks, May 2008.

ONE

Samuel Bignold

Sir Samuel Bignold was one of the great Victorian philanthropists. During his four periods of office as mayor, he did a great deal to help trade, industry and communications, and on top of that he ran a company whose name was synonymous with the city for years: Norwich Union.

He was born on 13 October 1791 in the parish of St Laurence in Norwich and he was the third son of Thomas Bignold, who was the founder of the Norwich Union insurance company. Thomas was known to be eccentric and very forthright in his remarks – one of his comments to someone who had heard that Norwich Union would insure any risk at a price and asked if he would insure against mad dogs was, 'No, because if you were to be bitten by a dog, I should not consider that the dog was mad.' Although Thomas was initially an able

Statue of Samuel Bignold outside the head office of Aviva, formerly Norwich Union, in Surrey Street. *(Photograph by author)*

secretary of both the Life and Fire Offices, his eccentricities grew more apparent. In 1806 he threatened directors with pistols when they disagreed with him, and he also started taking out expensive lawsuits against people whom he believed were claiming fraudulently. Some of them were fraudulent – but the number and cost of the lawsuits worried the policyholders. Norwich Union was a mutual company, owned by its policyholders, and eventually they rebelled against Thomas Bignold's behaviour and ousted him as secretary in 1818, electing his son Samuel in his place.

Bignold offered his father a generous retirement income, but Thomas's response was to initiate more lawsuits to overturn his dismissal. Meanwhile, Samuel Bignold moved from his country home to Bignold House in Surrey Street, which became both his private home and the headquarters of Norwich Union. Eventually Thomas became bankrupt in 1823 after his firm (which, incredibly, made and sold shoes with revolving heels) went under. He spent 16 months in the King's Bench prison before finally compromising with his son, who secured his release. Thomas then retired to Westerham until his death in 1835.

Bignold's main business interest was with the Fire Insurance Society. In the early 19th century, fire brigades had huge problems with discipline among their crews, particularly with drunkenness. Bignold tackled this by making rules about good conduct and not drinking, and his crews often went to help fight huge blazes in the city that weren't necessarily insured by Norwich Union, such as the inferno at the Cavalry Barracks in August 1843. He was also particular about his office staff; anyone who wanted to join the head office had to be clean shaven, a good writer and a Christian – though Bignold also insisted they had to be a Tory! He kept the Fire Insurance Society on a secure footing and when policyholders objected to low bonuses in 1837, claiming that Bignold's salary was too high and the headquarters should move to London rather than stay in Norwich, he met their challenges – and won.

In 1827, Bignold was unhappy when the private banks in the city announced that they would no longer pay interest on current accounts. He went one better than just moving his account; together with E.T. Booth and Mr Mercer, he set up the Norfolk and Norwich Joint Stock Banking Company. The bank failed in 1836 but its clients lost no money as he met all claims.

As well as overseeing huge growth in the business (his obituary in the *Eastern Daily Press* states that, under his management, a share of £30 became worth £275), Bignold took a lead role in civic affairs. He was elected a freeman of the city in June 1830, sheriff in August 1830 and was the mayor of Norwich in 1833, 1848, 1853 and 1872 – the first person since 1616 to be mayor three times, let alone four.

In his first mayoralty in 1833, he entertained 1,100 guests at the guild feast and 500 people at a ball in the Assembly House. However, it wasn't all jollity as the city was in the middle of an industrial crisis. One of the city's major trades was textiles, but falling production and increased competition led to a major recession. Many of the workers were forced to claim the poor rate and their families were suffering real hardship, but those paying the poor rate were also feeling the pinch and finding it difficult to pay their taxes. Bignold was aware of the needs of the

The Norwich Yarn Company mill in Whitefriars.
(Photograph by author)

community and established the Norwich Yarn Company in 1836, to spin yarn for the Norwich trade. Although the company eventually failed, it did help the city to weather the trade crisis.

Bignold recognised the importance of transport links; in September 1833 he opened Norwich as a port, and the following year he set up a provisional committee for the construction of a railway from Norwich to London – and then opened the Eastern Union Railway in 1849, during his second mayoralty.

As a person he was very popular; the *Illustrated London News* for 1855 summed him up by saying: 'He is himself a Conservative, but of a very moderate and Liberal cast; he is a general favourite with his fellow-citizens, from the probity of his conduct and the amenity of his manners.' He even managed to charm his political opponents; when a servant rushed in to warn him that the activist Daniel O'Connor was coming with a mob and suggested that he shut the gates against them, Bignold simply went to the door to meet O'Connor personally. The mob, instead of breaking his windows with the stones in their pockets, cheered him and went away again.

Bignold was knighted by Queen Victoria on 3 May 1854 after presenting an address to her on the subject of the war with Russia. He also supported the educational life of the city; he lent £4,000 to build the new library, of which he laid the first stone on 13 September 1854. The *Norfolk Chronicle* reported his speech:

> It has been my lot now, during my life, which has not been a short one, to aid a great many undertakings in this city – insurance offices, spinning factories, waterworks, literary and scientific institutions, and public charities; but I have never lent my assistance to any undertaking which more entirely commends itself to my judgement than that in which I am this day engaged in commencing.

As part of his mayoral duties that year, he also unveiled the statue of Wellington in the market place (which was moved to The Close in 1937).

He worked incredibly long hours, his dedication illustrated by the *Eastern Daily Press* who reported the 'singular trait in his character that he never seemed to desire a holiday'. He used to join his family on Saturday evening at Cromer, but would make sure he was back at Norwich Union for Monday morning. He also loved horse riding and would ride for an hour in the south of the city at 4pm each day.

On his 80th birthday, the clerks at Norwich Union gave him a 'massive silver inkstand in appreciation of the kindness and courtesy ever received from him'. That kindness and courtesy was extended further in his final mayoralty in 1872, when he gave a banquet especially for the elderly poor.

He died on 2 January 1875 and was buried in St Margaret's churchyard, Old Catton. On the day of his funeral, St Peter Mancroft's bell tolled, muffled, and the whole city was in mourning. The shops were all closed from 10am until 2pm as a mark of respect.

The local newspapers reported his funeral:

All the shops in the principal thoroughfares were either closed or shaded…hundreds of persons assembled in the market place…hundreds too, wearing the habiliments of mourning, were proceeding either to Surrey Street or to the Guildhall to take part in the procession of citizens…there were scores of carriages.

Clearly he was well liked and respected and, as the 'father of the city', very much mourned. On 6 January 1895 Norwich Corporation made a resolution of condolence to Bignold's family and stated 'their deep sense of the great loss the city has entertained by the death of one whose whole life was devoted to public business and to the benefit of all classes of his fellow citizen, especially those whose need in time of distress required help and sympathy'.

Today, Bignold is remembered most for his connections with Norwich Union. But he was more than just a businessman; he did what he could to help the citizens of the place he loved.

TWO

Thomas Bilney

Thomas Bilney was the first Protestant English martyr, and his preaching helped pave the way towards the Reformation of the church in the 16th century. He was born about 1495, probably in the village of Bilney near Dereham. He was known as 'Little Bilney' because he was short and slender. Bilney went to Cambridge in 1510 to read law at Trinity Hall and was ordained as a priest at Ely in September 1519. He became a Fellow at Trinity Hall in 1524 and also held the office of university proctor, being responsible for discipline at the university. However, he fell foul of the authorities in a big way and ended up burned at the stake in Norwich.

Thomas Bilney being pulled from the pulpit at Ipswich, from *The Acts and Monuments* of John Foxe, fourth edition, 1877. *(Photograph by author)*

The politics of the Tudor period were heavily bound up with religion, and Thomas was caught in the middle of it as an early advocate of reform. In 1516 he read Erasmus's translation of the New Testament and was very struck by the phrase of St Paul in I Timothy 1:15 – 'It is a true saying, and worthy of all men to be embraced, that Christ Jesus came into the world to save sinners, of whom I am the chief and principal.' If Paul, who thought himself the chief sinner, could be saved, then Bilney realised that he could be saved too. He is recorded as saying that when he read the passage he 'felt a marvellous comfort and quietness'.

At this point Bilney realised that the relics and images offered by the clergy, particularly monasteries, were set up for the financial benefit of the institutions, not for the souls of the people who paid for the images. Merle d'Aubigné, an early biographer, quotes Bilney saying, 'I see it all: my vigils, my fasts, my pilgrimages, my purchase of masses and indulgences, were destroying me instead of saving me. All these efforts were, as St Augustine says, a hasty running out of the right way.' As a result, Bilney became very ascetic; he didn't sleep much and ate very simple food. He also loathed music, especially the recorder-playing of his neighbour, Dr Thirlby (later the bishop of Norwich), about which he complained bitterly, though it isn't noted whether Thirlby played particularly badly! He converted others to his beliefs, notably Hugh Latimer, who was later one of the leading spokesmen for the Reformation and was chaplain to Henry VIII.

In July 1525 Bilney was licensed to preach in the diocese of Ely. His sermons attracted the attention of the authorities, but when he was brought up before Cardinal Wolsey the cardinal was lenient and merely made him swear an oath not to preach Lutheran heresy. Two years later Bilney was preaching again – this time against pilgrimages to the shrine at Walsingham, worshipping saints and leaving offerings before images and relics. He said, 'The cowl of St Francis wrapped round a dead body hath no power to take away sins.' This seems very obvious to modern eyes, but in the 16th century it was believed that the way to get to heaven was to do good works, fast, do purgatory and attend mass – all of which meant paying money to the church.

Although Bilney was orthodox in his views on the power of the Pope, the sacrifice of the Mass, the doctrine of transubstantiation and the authority of the church, he went too far for the authorities when he urged the king to smash all the images; he was later dragged from the pulpit at St George's Church in Ipswich and arrested. He appeared before Cardinal Wolsey in November 1527 and said that Luther was 'a wicked and detestable heretic', so Wolsey was appeased and appointed Bishop Tunstal of London to preside over the rest of the trial. Bilney then claimed that he couldn't remember what he'd said in his sermons.

Most people thought that Bilney wasn't a heretic and the whole thing was set up by the friars after he had criticised their greed in his sermons, but at the end of the trial he was put in the Tower of London. His sentence was deferred until he recanted his heretical views, and he was consequently kept in the tower for over a year.

According to John Foxe, the author of the *Book of Martyrs*, Bilney then made a statement renouncing 'all manner of heresies and articles following whereupon I am now defamed, noted, vehemently suspected and convicted'. It is recorded that the Lord Chancellor Thomas More was surprised by the result of the trial because he'd realised that Bilney hadn't admitted to preaching heresy.

Bilney was finally let out of prison in 1529, but his retraction of his views weighed on his conscience, and his friends were so worried about him that one of them stayed with him at all hours of the day or night in case he tried to kill himself.

In 1531 he travelled to Norwich, where he resorted to preaching in the open air as he didn't have a licence to do so in churches. He renounced his earlier recantation of his beliefs and distributed copies of Tyndale's English translation of the New Testament, which had been banned by the authorities. He may have given a copy of the book to Katherine Manne, the anchoress at Blackfriars in St Andrew's; she was walled up there at her own request, so she could devote her life to God and counsel others. He then travelled to London and was arrested in March 1532. The authorities returned him to Norwich as a prisoner, and Bishop Nix's officers convicted him as a relapsed heretic.

Bilney appealed to the king as the supreme head of the church, but Thomas Pelles, the chancellor of Norwich diocese, refused to let the appeal go through. So Bilney was condemned to be burned as a heretic and was imprisoned in Norwich Guildhall.

The night before his execution, according to John Foxe's *Book of Martyrs*, Bilney held his finger in the candle flame for so long that he burned it down to the first joint. When one of his companions asked what he was doing, he said, 'Nothing but trying my flesh by God's grace, and burning one joint. Tomorrow God's rods shall burn my whole body in the fire.'

On 19 August 1531 he was led through Norwich from the Guildhall and taken across Bishop's Bridge to the Lollards' Pit. He gave alms via his friends on his way. A large sympathetic crowd gathered there, including Matthew Parker.

Bilney fell to his knees, prayed, then embraced the stake and kissed it. Thomas Pelles, the chancellor, gave Bilney a written recantation which he read silently. Bilney then recited the creed and told the crowd he regretted preaching without a licence (though he didn't mention regretting the contents of his sermons). Several of the friars told him they were worried about a backlash against them by people sympathetic to him, so he added that the friars weren't responsible for his death. He denied that he'd taught heresy,

The Guildhall, where Thomas Bilney spent his last days. *(Photograph by author)*

stated he was a Catholic, and then reeds were put around him, the fire was lit and he was burned at the stake. Horribly, according to both Foxe and Blomefield, the flames were blown away from him three times, meaning that he roasted before the fire finally consumed him.

There was a huge political row afterwards and Thomas More examined both the city MP Edward Reed and the city alderman John Curatt. Both gave different stories; Reed said Bilney hadn't admitted to being a heretic, while Curatt said Bilney had admitted heresy. However, Curatt gave the most improbable excuse for not hearing the actual words: he claimed he hadn't heard exactly what Bilney said because he'd stooped to tie his shoelaces. More realised that he wasn't going to get any further with the investigation and gave up.

In the *Book of Martyrs*, published in 1554, John Foxe made a case for Bilney to be considered a martyr:

Plaque to Thomas Bilney on the Guildhall. *(Photograph by author)*

There was never a more innocent and upright man in all England then he was...he converted his study to those things which tended more unto godliness than profit...there was in his heart an incredible desire to allure many unto the gospel, desiring nothing more, then that he might stir up and encourage any to the love of Christ and sincere godliness.

However, Bilney didn't see himself as a martyr; he simply stressed the importance of personal faith and criticised the abuses of the mediaeval penitential system. Foxe also reported Bishop Nix as commenting after the burning, 'By God's mother I fear I have burned Abel, and let Cain go.' In 1534 Nix was condemned on a charge of executing Bilney without authorisation from the state, and his property was confiscated. He was, however, still buried in the cathedral.

Bilney is remembered today by a plaque on the Guildhall.

THREE

George Borrow

A fine old city, truly, is that, view it from whatever side you will, but it shows best from the east, where the ground, bold and elevated, overlooks the fair and fertile valley in which it stands.

(George Borrow on Norwich, from *Lavengro*)

George Borrow. *(Photograph by kind permission of Barrett & Coe)*

George Henry Borrow was one of the best-known 19th-century authors from Norwich. He was, however, more than just the creator of the city's motto. He was a larger-than-life character, an adventurer with a wild streak who courted danger and yet, at the same time, desperately needed the acceptance of people around him.

He was born on 5 July 1803 at East Dereham in the house of his mother's parents. His father, Captain Thomas Borrow of the West Norfolk militia, was a professional soldier, so Borrow's childhood was spent travelling around with his father's regiment.

Borrow was a lonely child, stating he was 'ever conscious of a peculiar heaviness within me, and at times of a strange sensation of fear, which occasionally amounted to horror, and for which I could assign no real cause whatever.' These 'horrors' would continue to dog him throughout his life.

When Borrow was 10 years old, his parents moved to Yaxley near Peterborough. There he became friendly with a viper-catcher and herbalist, who gave him a viper he had tamed and from which he'd removed the fangs. Borrow used to carry the viper around with him and fed it milk. This later gave rise to a legend when Borrow met an encampment of gypsies nearby and had an altercation with them – the snake apparently lifted its head from Borrow's shoulders and glared at them. The gypsies were amazed and called him 'a *sap-engro*, a chap who catches snakes, and plays tricks with them' – and soon after this Borrow became friends with their son Ambrose Petulengro (whom he calls 'Jasper' in his semi-autobiographical works *Lavengro* and *The Romany Rye*).

Borrow liked to see himself as a man of mystery. The first chapter of *Lavengro* tells a story, supposedly from his own childhood, when he was drawing lines in the dust, and a Jewish pedlar who was watching him nearby paled on seeing what Borrow had drawn: 'taking off his hat, he made some strange gestures to me, cringing, chattering...and shortly departed, muttering something about "holy letters", and talking to himself in a strange tongue.'

In July 1814 the Borrows moved back to Norwich and stayed at the Crown and Angel in St Stephen's Street. Borrow went to Norwich Grammar School from 1814 to 1815, while his elder brother John studied painting with John Crome. Borrow absolutely hated school, although later his former schoolmate Dr James Martineau said that even at school Borrow had a gift for telling stories and would gather three or four of his schoolfellows, tell them a story and illustrate it.

In 1815 Borrow's father and his regiment had a spell in Ireland; the family went too, and Borrow continued to tell stories to people. He also learned to ride and his lifelong love of horses dated from this period.

The following year the family went back to Norwich and settled in Willow Lane. But Borrow, to his dismay, was sent back to Norwich Grammar School. He was described as 'unruly', and he ran away – an adventure which was a typical Borrovian tale of derring-do. He persuaded three other boys to join him on a trip to Caister, saying that they would find a cave to live in and earn money by working for smugglers. The parents of another schoolfriend found them at Acle and fed them; naturally, the hungry schoolboys were happy to tuck into a good meal after their long walk. But meanwhile the adults sent word to Edward Valpy, the headmaster, who fetched them back and whipped Borrow in front of the whole school.

After that, Borrow preferred to educate himself outside school. He bought grammars in second-hand shops and studied French and Italian with Revd Thomas D'Eterville in St Locket's Yard off St Andrew's. Borrow called him 'one banished priest' and there were rumours that D'Eterville dealt in contraband and carried a pistol – just the kind of adventurous characteristics that would appeal to Borrow. Borrow also learnt boxing from John Thurtell (who was hanged in 1824 for murder); he was fascinated by pugilism and watched the famous fight between Ned Painter and Tom Oliver in North Walsham in 1820. If anyone asked him the secret of a quiet life, his response was, 'Learn to box, and keep a civil tongue in your head.' Interestingly, although his father never encouraged him in his love of pugilism, Thomas Borrow had a reputation as an excellent boxer.

Borrow continued his education until 1818, when depression set in again. He referred to it as 'the horrors', and when his mother asked him what he was afraid of, he replied, 'Of nothing I can express...mine is a dread of I know not what, and there the horror lies.'

His father was less sympathetic to what he saw as a difficult boy who spent his time idling round with unsavoury characters, and in March 1819 Captain Borrow arranged for him to be apprenticed to the solicitor and town clerk William Simpson in Tuck's Court, off St Giles's Street. Borrow actually spent most of his time on Mousehold Heath, talking to the gypsies and prize fighters there, as well as studying many different languages in the Corporation library. He threatened to knock down Simpson's other clerks if they teased the Welsh ostler in Tuck's Court and, in return, the ostler taught him Welsh.

Borrow's translations were published posthumously in 16 volumes in Norwich, in 1923, and it is thought that he had some knowledge (either reading or writing) of around 100 languages. One of his tutors was the writer and revolutionary William Taylor, who taught him German and a bit of Danish. Taylor was impressed enough to write to his friend Robert Southey, the poet laureate, 'though not yet eighteen, [he] understands 12 languages'.

Taylor persuaded Borrow to consider earning his living by writing, and some of his translations appeared in Sir Richard Phillips's *Monthly Magazine*. In 1824, a month after his father's death and two days after his articles had expired, Borrow moved to London with the intention of becoming a man of letters. He soon discovered it wasn't that easy. He lived on bread and water for a while and spent a year in Grub Street, compiling six volumes of *Celebrated Trials* for Phillips and writing articles, but was penniless and became depressed again. He even wrote to his friend Roger Kerrison: 'Come to me immediately; I am, I believe, dying.' He wasn't – and then he spent a few years wandering around England as a tinker and horse dealer, teaching himself how to shoe horses. During this period he kept returning to Norwich – because Norfolk was where 'the people eat the

George Borrow's house off Willow Lane. *(Photograph by author)*

best dumplings in the world, and speak the purest English'.

In 1833 the British and Foreign Bible Society, who had heard about Borrow's linguistic ability, offered him an interview for a job. He couldn't afford to travel to London, so he walked there. It took him 27 hours, and he later said that his outlay was five shillings and five pence for one pint of ale, half a pint of milk, a roll of bread, and two apples. At the interview, the Society was impressed by his ability with languages (and also by him physically – Borrow was 6ft 3in and his hair had turned completely grey before he was 20) and hired him. Borrow spent six months learning Manchu before the Society sent him to St Petersburg to oversee the printing of the New Testament in Manchu. After St Petersburg, they sent him to Portugal and Spain to distribute scriptures.

Spain was a huge adventure for Borrow. At the time, Spain was in the grip of the Carlist wars (fought between the supporters of the infant queen Isabella II and the supporters of her uncle Carlos V, a 'pretender' who tried to claim the throne in succession from his brother Ferdinand VII), so it was a dangerous place to live. He spent a great deal of his time riding a black Andalucian stallion and translated the Bible into Romany. He ended up in jail three times after clashing with the authorities – and was almost shot as a spy.

In 1839 Borrow rented a house in Seville; an old family friend, Mary Clarke, joined him there with her daughter Henriette. The following year Borrow finally returned to London and married Mary three weeks later. The family settled in Mary's estate in Oulton Broad and Borrow began to write. First came *Zincali,* in 1841, about the Spanish gypsies. *The Bible In Spain,* his account of five years spent in the Peninsula, followed in 1843 and was a huge success; it sold almost 20,000 copies in a year (nearly three times the sales of the first edition of Dickens's *Pickwick Papers*) and went into six editions in the first year alone.

Then depression set in again, and in 1844 Borrow travelled alone across Europe to Constantinople and started writing *Lavengro*. The book, which he called 'a dream of study and adventure', was published in 1851 and was followed six years later by *Romany Rye* (1857). Both books are about journeys, interspersed with travellers' tales, and it's difficult to tell which part is autobiographical, which is fiction and which is descriptive travel writing. The books did not sell anywhere near as well as *The Bible in Spain* (partly due to a change in public taste and partly because he had let too long pass between books instead of capitalising on his success) and his reputation declined after that.

In 1853 Borrow and his family moved to Great Yarmouth, and here he had a chance to be a hero. On 8 September a storm whipped up the waves and a barge nearly capsized. Borrow walked straight into the high seas and rescued the man who had been

Plaque to George Borrow at Willow Lane. *(Photograph by author)*

washed overboard. He also claimed to newspaper reporters that he was the only one in deep water and the beachmen at Yarmouth hadn't gone in as far as he had.

He spent the next few years on walking tours in Norfolk, Cornwall, Wales, the Isle of Man, Scotland and Ireland – all the time carrying his battered green umbrella, and not put off in the least by stormy weather. He moved to Brompton with his family in 1860, and published *Wild Wales* in 1862; *Celtic Bards, Chiefs and Kings* was also written during this period, although it wasn't published until 1928.

Borrow's wife Mary died on 30 January 1869 – her death certificate lists the cause as 'valvular disease of the heart and dropsy' – and she was buried in Brompton Cemetery. During her last days, Borrow had the 'horrors' again, and Mary's doctor commented that he thought Borrow had 'a very aggravated form of hysteria' or a serious mental affection and that Mary didn't get the careful nursing she needed.

Borrow was completely lost and lonely without Mary – she had written letters for him, stopped him getting the 'horrors', and kept an eye on his finances. He proposed to Lucy Brightwell, a writer and etcher who had been a childhood friend in Norwich, but she declined. He wrote *Romano Lavo-Lil*, published in 1874; the book was badly received by Romany scholars and was the only one that wasn't profitable in his lifetime. Borrow's response was that he was going back to East Anglia to die.

On his return to Norfolk, Borrow lived in Oulton but spent much of his time in Norwich drinking at the Norfolk Hotel (later the site of the Hippodrome and now

St Giles's car park), or walking around Oulton with a sheepdog. Being Borrow, he had no ordinary dog – his sheepdog had a squint! The villagers were a little scared of him, particularly children, as he tended to sing to himself in strange languages as he walked around with his dog. The saddest part is that Borrow loved children and would have really enjoyed telling them his stories and adventures.

Mary's daughter Henriette came to live in Oulton with her husband to look after Borrow, but she wasn't very organised and the house became a complete tip. In 1879 she told one enquirer that Borrow couldn't walk as far as the garden gate. Borrow was becoming more querulous with age; when the vicar of Lowestoft asked him how old he was, he snapped, 'Sir, I tell my age to no man.'

He made his will in December 1880, leaving everything to Henriette in trust for the daughter of a fellow clerk from his days as Simpson's apprentice; Borrow loathed Henriette's husband and didn't want him to be able to inherit any of the estate.

On 22 July 1881 Henriette and her husband went to Lowestoft on business for a few days. Borrow wasn't happy about them leaving him, and they returned to find that he had died on 26 July from 'decay of nature'. He was buried next to his beloved Mary at Brompton Cemetery on 4 August, and by then he had been practically forgotten as a literary lion.

However, in the decade after his death, his reputation grew again; the city celebrated his centenary in 1913 (10 years late!) and Arthur Samuel, the lord mayor at the time, bought Borrow House and donated it to the city as a museum.

Henry Beeching preached a sermon about Borrow at the Cathedral on 6 July 1913 and described him as:

> A true seer and interpreter; because he opened to us fresh springs of delight in the natural world; because he aroused new and living interest in the lives of men of many kindreds and tongues; and because he held up to our own nation an ideal of conduct which could not but benefit those whom it attracted.

But perhaps the last word on Borrow should come from *Lavengro,* spoken by the gypsy on Mousehold Heath: 'There's night and day, brother, both sweet things; sun, moon, and stars, brother, all sweet things; there's likewise a wind on the heath. Life is very sweet, brother.'

FOUR

Sir Thomas Browne

Portrait of Sir Thomas Browne. *(Photograph by author, by kind permission of St Peter Mancroft Church)*

Sir Thomas Browne was truly a Renaissance man; he was renowned as a doctor, an author, a herbalist, a botanist, a naturalist, a linguist and a collector. Nowadays he's remembered in the city for his statue on Hay Hill and the recent art installation; however, the man behind the statue was fascinating.

He was born in the parish of St Michael-le-Querne in Cheapside, London, on 19 October 1605. He had four sisters and was the only son of Thomas Browne, a liveryman of the Mercers' Company of London, and his wife Anne Garraway.

Thomas Browne senior died in November 1613, and a few months later Anne married the courtier Sir Thomas Dutton, to whom she had lent money out of the estate. Dutton was so extravagant that the court of aldermen actually had to step in to stop Dutton and his wife completely wasting the inheritance of the five Browne children. Their uncle Edward Browne administered the estate from then on, so there was enough money for Thomas Browne to go to Winchester College at the University of Oxford in 1616.

In 1623 Browne matriculated at Broadgates Hall (nowadays known as Pembroke College). He took his MA in 1629, then studied in Montpellier and

Padua before graduating as an MD in Leiden in 1633. After graduation he went back to England, where he was apprenticed (according to different sources) either at Oxford or Halifax. When Thomas Dutton died, Browne went to visit his mother in Ireland and started writing arguably his most famous work, *Religio Medici*, from 1635–36.

He moved to Norwich in 1636 on the advice of Revd Thomas Lushington, his old tutor at Oxford, who had moved to the city himself in 1635. In 1641, aged 36, Browne married 20-year-old Dorothy Mileham and established East Anglia's leading medical practice.

Statue of Sir Thomas Browne in the Haymarket. *(Photograph by author)*

In 1642 *Religio Medici* was published in London without his permission, so he prepared an authorised edition of his own in 1643. This was an exploration of his own religion, and he summed it up as: 'I could never divide myself from any man upon the difference of an opinion...persecution is a bad and indirect way to plant religion.'

Between 1643 and 1649 the Browne family lived in the Upper King Street and Tombland area of the city, where he wrote *Pseudodoxia Epidemica* (sometimes known as 'Vulgar Errors') – which details erroneous folk beliefs and the truth behind them.

In 1949 the Brownes moved to the Haymarket. There is a plaque on the site of his house at 5 Orford Place; his house was converted firstly to a china warehouse, then demolished in 1842 and a bank built in its stead (which in turn was demolished in 1892 to make room for the trams). The statue on Hay Hill, by Henry Pegram, looks towards the spot where his house once was.

Many people visited Browne for 'his admirable skill in physick', and Browne always felt that his first duty was being a doctor. He visited his patients across the region by coach and horseback and didn't charge the poor for treating them. Most of his prescriptions were herbal pharmaceutics (quinine and opium were the only effective drugs of the period), and he grew most of the herbs in his own garden –

the diarist John Evelyn visited in 1671 and said that Browne's 'whole house and garden being a paradise and cabinet of rarities, and that of the best collection, specially medals, books, plants and natural things'. (He owned over 2,000 books, and he also collected maps and birds' eggs.)

The physician Sir William Osler told his medical students in London that they could learn three lessons from Browne's life: 'mastery of self, conscientious devotion to duty, deep interest in human beings'. The Fellows of the Royal College of Physicians in London elected Browne to an honorary fellowship of the college in 1664, and his diploma describes him as 'virtute et literis ornitassimum Virum' (a man eminently endowed with virtue and literature). He continued to write and in 1658 published a book entitled *Urne-Burial*, a book about customs.

Browne was held in high esteem by his fellow citizens. John Whitefoot describes him in *Some Minutes for the Life of Sir Thomas Browne*:

> His Complexion and Hair was answerable to his Name, his Stature was moderate, and Habit of Body neither fat nor lean...he had an Aversion to all Finery, and affected Plainness, both in the Fashion and Ornaments...His Memory...was Capacious and Tenacious...he was Excellent Company when he was at leisure.

He was clearly quite a serious man as Whitefoot continues that Browne was cheerful but 'rarely merry' and seldom cracked a joke – and blushed when he did! He also worked very hard; Whitefoot asserts that Browne was:

> ...parsimonious in nothing but his Time, whereof he made as much Improvement, with as little Loss as any Man in it; when he had any to spare from his drudging Practice, he was scarce patient of any Diversion from his Study; so impatient of Sloth and Idleness, that he would say, he could not do nothing.

As well as being a physician, writer and philosopher, Browne was also renowned for his work as a naturalist. He made notes on the birds, fishes and plants of Norfolk, and was one of the first to write about the migratory habits of birds; he kept a bittern in his garden for two years as part of his studies. He also performed the first experiments in embryology, and his interest in antiquarian matters led him to catalogue the monuments in Norwich Cathedral.

As a writer, he was incredibly innovative and added a great many new words to the dictionary – including words we take for granted today such as electricity, hallucination, ambidextrous, cylindrical, inconsistent, poisonously, polarity and typographer. Many of his sayings are now well-known aphorisms – such as 'Charity begins at home.' He also collected words of Norfolk dialect, such as mawther, bunny (meaning a bruise or swelling) and stingy (in the sense of mean). Interestingly, he also forecast the end of the world in the year 7000.

His hard work was recognised by the king. On 29 September 1671 Charles II was going to knight the mayor, Thomas Thacker, but Thacker declined the honour and instead the king knighted 65-year-old Browne at St Andrew's Hall. Soon after, Browne was dissecting a dolphin and sent the 'collars' to the king at Newmarket, as his wife Dorothy had 'an art to dresse & cooke the flesh so as to make an excellent savoury dish'.

In the last few weeks of his life, Browne suffered from stomach pains and a fever. He died on his 77th birthday, 19 October 1682, and was buried in St Peter Mancroft. He left his house in the Haymarket to his wife and his books to his eldest son, Edward, who became a noted doctor in London.

But Browne's story doesn't end there. In 1840 Mary Bowman, the wife of the pastor of St Peter Mancroft, died. While her grave was being dug, Browne's coffin was accidentally broken by workmen, and Robert Fitch, a chemist who became the churchwarden of St Peter Mancroft five years later, took the skull and coffin plate. Fitch meant to put them back, but by the time he returned the skull it was too late as Browne's grave had already been sealed again. In 1845 the skull passed to Dr Edward Lubbock, who gave the skull to the museum of the Norfolk and Norwich hospital. It remained there until 1922, when William Osler (the Regius Professor of Medicine at the University of Oxford) had the skull examined by the Royal College of Surgeons in London and then finally returned Browne's skull to the church. The skull was reinterred just below his memorial at a special service on 4 July 1922, and a copy of the skull is still on display in the vestry.

Cast of Sir Thomas Browne's skull. *(Photograph by author, by kind permission of St Peter Mancroft Church)*

FIVE

Edward Burgess

Edward Burgess is one of the city's characters who could be a hero or a villain, depending on your viewpoint. According to the ruling classes, Burgess was a troublemaker who told lies and stirred up discontent – and he certainly spent a lot of time in the magistrates' court. But people in the city loved him because he supported the poor and exposed lies.

Burgess was born in Norwich on 21 June 1846; his father died on Christmas Eve 1852, leaving a widow and five children totally unsupported. His mother was a gifted nurse and worked for William Cadge, but she struggled for money and his family was too poor to give him more than three years of education. He spent all his spare time with a textbook in his hand, but meanwhile he worked in the packing room at Colman's. When the family moved to Cheshire, Burgess became an insurance superintendent. He married, taking an oath at his wedding never to touch strong drink, then moved back to Norwich and opened the Livingstone Hotel in St Giles in 1875, the first Temperance Hotel in the city. In the 1878 floods Burgess was one of the first to offer shelter to the victims, and he housed and fed 38 people for a week, clothing some of them as well.

In 1878 Burgess published the first issue of the *Daylight*, a weekly journal which he said would expose villainy, humbug and fraud. The first issue sold out very quickly, and in most issues he put pressure on the authorities to sort out the disorderly pubs in Ber Street and the brothels in Dove Lane and Cow Hill. He collected the issues as an almanac every year, and his co-publisher was Mr Burgis – a name very close to his own. He was often in court on charges of libel, and in every single court case it was asked whether they were talking about Mr Burgess with an E or Mr Burgis with an I; the newspapers report that this caused much amusement to the spectators.

However, Burgess was more than just the publisher of a satirical paper; he also did a lot of work on behalf of the poorer people in Norwich. In 1878 he became a member of the Board of Guardians, and in 1880 he was elected to the School Board – very clearly the favoured candidate as he polled 10,000 votes. And he kept his election expenses low, too – the local papers noted that he kept them to under £4 10s. For a while he was the vice-chair of the board.

In 1882 Burgess stood for election as an Independent politician; his friends were worried that he might lose the election to become a councillor for the Sixth Ward, so they also ran a campaign on his behalf in the Seventh Ward. However, Burgess won in both wards.

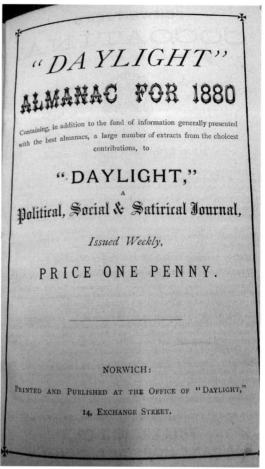

Cover of the 1880 almanac. *(Photograph by author)*

Clearly he couldn't be a councillor for two wards at once, so he resigned from the Seventh Ward.

He also did much for the poor in the hard winter of 1889. In February 1889 he organised the Voluntary Unemployed Bread Fund and appointed a committee from the unemployed workers, setting up the headquarters at St Stephen's Hall. He collected between £300 and £400 to help support the poor and also talked tradesmen into contributing bread, meat, vegetables and clothing.

In 1894 he and Alderman Wild set up the first Norwich Cabmen's dinner; Burgess collected the funds and made the arrangements for every dinner until the one just before his death.

The *Norfolk Chronicle* said in his obituary:

> A man of strong and decided views, he was absolutely fearless in advocating them; those to whom he was most strenuously opposed never doubted his conscientiousness and will most sincerely sympathise with those who mourn his decease.

He was definitely fearless – he was absolutely opposed to vaccination (it's easy to imagine how he would have reacted to the MMR scare of the early 21st century), and only one of his seven children was vaccinated. Eventually he was fined £50 for refusing to have his children vaccinated – and he was summoned so many times that he made the papers into a reel...which was an incredible 60ft long.

But where he really fell foul of the authorities was over what he published in the *Daylight*. On Valentine's Day 1883 solicitor Joseph Stanley came running up to Burgess in London Street demanding to know if he had published 'certain statements' in the *Daylight* (headed 'Wanted: a Pedigree'). When Burgess said yes, Stanley took a whip from inside his coat and lashed Burgess over the face – one witness claimed that Stanley boasted later about reducing Burgess's face to 'a gridiron'. Stanley freely admitted to horsewhipping Burgess, even writing a letter to say so, but he claimed it was justified because Burgess was a rogue who had defamed his father-in-law Mr Gilman, the mayor of the city. When Burgess took him to court, the magistrates' court was absolutely packed, with many solicitors and council members in attendance.

Burgess's lawyer Mr Blofeld was eloquent in court:

> This is not a question of whether you approve of the different writings that from time to time appear in the *Daylight*...whether they are in good taste, or are calculating to offend the natural susceptibility of the people of Norwich is neither here not there in the inquiry...It may be all very well to cowhide an editor in San Francisco, but an outrage of this kind in the streets of Norwich will, I am sure, never be tolerated by the magistrates of this city.

He went further in saying that Stanley's attack was cowardly as the solicitor had hidden the whip until the last moment. When the magistrates asked Burgess if he had had anything to use in defending himself against Stanley's attack, Burgess answered cheerfully that he had a rolled-up umbrella and 'used it to the best advantage'. In the end, PC Middleton and the people who had gathered to watch the spectacle had to put them on opposite sides of the street. Stanley's lawyer, Mr Browne, was just as scathing about Burgess: 'What peace it must bring to a man at the last, to earn his daily pence by vilifying those who are honourable and true and just, and wish to do the best they can for their fellow-citizens.'

Various statements published in the *Daylight* were held up to scrutiny, including the case Burgess had stated about the bishop living the life of luxury in his palace while one of his poor neighbours had died in filth and squalor, shoved in a coffin that was too small for him. The magistrates barely even retired to consider their verdict; they fined Stanley a mere shilling for assault and refused to give costs to Burgess.

The fact that Stanley had got off so lightly opened the gates for more complaints against Burgess. A week later William Hammond of E. Field and Co. claimed he had been libelled by the *Daylight*. He had originally submitted the case to the High Court, asking for damages of £1,000, but the case was sent back to the county court when Hammond failed to give security for court costs. Partway through the hearing Hammond's own lawyer said he didn't think it was right to ask the jury for damages, so Burgess won the case.

A couple of days later, on 24 February, artist Arthur Ventnor of Bridewell Alley was in the dock for breaking the plate-glass windows of the *Daylight*'s offices and causing £20 of damage after they had exhibited a caricature of him. The city recorder (W.J. Meltcalfe) said that Ventnor had had considerable provocation and would be sentenced to be imprisoned for three hours, but as he had already spent more than that time in the dock he would be discharged, and 'people who provoke other people to smash their windows' (i.e. the *Daylight*) should pay the costs of prosecution.

There was another libel case on 23 April – this one much nastier – from Lewin Samuel, a clothier of St Giles's Street. The *Daylight* claimed that Samuel and his brother were money lenders and extorted more than 150 per cent annual interest for small loans. The *Daylight* absolutely refused to print advertisements for money lenders in their pages (interestingly, the judge commended them for that), and, from the details that came out, a brother who said he took 'no active part' in the business admitted that he would do anything that Lewin Samuel asked him to do – which didn't impress the judge. One witness said that she had borrowed

£33 and repaid £51 10s, yet 11 months later the Samuels put in an execution for £66 6s – which appears to be a phenomenal amount of interest. Various customers signed bills of sale without knowing what they were signing for, and their goods were seized – including bedding. Halfway through the case – after a lot of examples like this had been aired – Samuels suddenly decided to withdraw.

There was still a long-running fight between Burgess and Stanley, with 'Obadiah' (probably Burgess, although he refused to admit it in court in case it would 'criminate' him) writing many things in the *Daylight* about Stanley, and Stanley responding with a libel action. In 1886 Burgess was up before the magistrates at the assizes in Ipswich, charged with libel yet again by Stanley. He was sentenced to three months in prison, but on his release on 3 August there was a huge popular demonstration at Thorpe Station. Twenty-five thousand people cheered him wildly, and several of the more enthusiastic supporters took the horses from his carriage and dragged it all the way up the hill from the station to his home in Surrey Street. Later, he gave a two-hour talk in St Andrew's Hall, entitled 'My Prison Experience' – and it was packed. On several occasions funds for his defence in court were set up by his friends, and many people subscribed to them.

The *Norwich Mercury* described him as an 'Angel of Discord' in 1891 (quite rich from a paper that was the equivalent of a red-top!), but his health was failing and eventually the *Daylight* faded and became an annual diary.

Burgess died on 3 March 1911 at his house near St Stephen's Gate, at the age of 65.

SIX

Edith Cavell

Monument of Edith Cavell outside the cathedral. *(Photograph by author)*

Edith Cavell is remembered today as the nurse who became a martyr in World War One, shot by the Germans for helping Allied soldiers. However, she had a much bigger impact than that on the nursing profession, both in England and in Europe.

Edith Louisa Cavell was born in Swardeston on 4 December 1865, the first of Revd Frederick Cavell and his wife Louisa's four children. She was taught at home in the rectory by her parents, and her father taught her three important principles which lasted her whole life and also contributed to her death – thought for others, self-sacrifice and prayer.

She was sent to school, first of all in 1883 to Belgrave House School in Clevedon, then to London, and finally to Laurel Court in Peterborough. When she left school Cavell became the governess to the family of the vicar of Steeple Bumpstead in Essex. She then inherited some money and used it to travel; with the recommendation of Margaret Gibson, the headmistress of Laurel Court, she became governess to the François family in Belgium and stayed with them for six years.

In 1895 Cavell came back to England to nurse her father, who was seriously ill. Over the next year she realised that nursing was her vocation, and when her father was better she decided to train as a nurse, despite the fact that, at almost 31 years of age, she was quite old to be a student. She started at the London Hospital School of Nursing in Whitechapel Road in September 1896 and was one of six nurses seconded to help with the typhoid epidemic in Maidstone – only 132 of the 1,700 people who caught it died, and Edith received the Maidstone Medal for her work. Eva Lückes, the matron – who never gave good reports – criticised her work, saying that Cavell was unpunctual, was not 'very much in earnest', could not 'altogether be depended on' and would have been a better nurse if she had put her whole heart into it.

In the years to come Cavell was to prove those reports completely wrong. She was also very keen on punctuality in her nurses – any nurse more than two minutes late for breakfast would forfeit two hours of her own time.

In 1901 Cavell became the night superintendent at the St Pancras Infirmary, a Poor Law hospital. Two years later she became the assistant matron of Shoreditch Infirmary, which had 750 beds in the wards and 120 nurses for her to supervise. She also pioneered follow-up visits by going to see patients after she had discharged them. She had a reputation for having a great sense of duty and being kind to poor and sick, but at the same time she was very reserved and could be a bit humourless.

Her love of travelling resurfaced in 1906, and she ended up in Belgium. Dr Antoine De Page wanted to reduce the influence of the religious orders on caring for the sick so he could introduce new techniques and improve medical care, so he set up the Berkendael Institute, a training school and clinic in Brussels. In 1907 he appointed Cavell as its first matron; although she was the director, she had to report to De Page and the committees. She recruited staff from London, and her constant companion was her Jack Russell terrier, Jack.

The first certificates of competence were awarded in 1910, and Cavell improved the standard of nursing at the institute. Her reputation grew, enabling her to make huge changes to the working lives of nurses. At the time, nurses' duties included cleaning as well as caring for the sick; Cavell insisted that private nurses should be treated on a par with the family and not as servants, and she managed to get doctors to respect nurses and see them as professionals and not just cleaners. From 1910 state registration of nurses was introduced, and a new hospital opened in the St Gilles district of Brussels. By 1912 she was providing nurses for three hospitals, 24 communal schools and 13 kindergartens, and by 1914 she was giving four lectures a week to nurses and doctors.

After lectures, Cavell used to play the piano to her students; however, she was clearly still very focused on work because in later years her students never remembered her singing or smiling while she played. She had planned to expand the training programme at the institute, and a new hospital was planned in St Gilles, but building work had to stop when German forces occupied Belgium in 1914.

Following the assassination of Archduke Franz Ferdinand in July 1914, Cavell returned briefly to Norwich to see her mother. War was declared, and Cavell could have stayed in Britain or joined a field hospital, but she felt that her duty was to go back to Brussels with her nurses. She returned to Brussels on 3 August, the day before Britain declared war on Germany, and wrote to *The Times* asking people to subscribe to the Red Cross hospitals for the wounded army soldiers.

The Berkendael Institute became a Red Cross hospital, and Brussels was invaded by Germany on 19 August. Cavell wrote to the *Nursing Mirror*, saying that some of the German soldiers thought they were in Paris and did not understand what quarrel they had with the Belgians. She saw the soldiers 'pick up little children and give them chocolate and seat them on their horses, and some had tears in their eyes at the recollection of their little ones at home'. Along with other English nurses in Brussels Cavell was offered safe conduct to Holland but, believing that her duties lay with her patients and colleagues, she refused.

When Baron von Bissing was assigned as the military governor of Belgium he instigated a rule that any male patients over the age of 18 had to report to the German military police when discharged from hospital; the patient would then be sent to the labour camp. Cavell and her nurses would tell any such patient to go to the police, but would then add that instead he could go to the home of 'Madame X', (where he would be hidden until he could be safely guided out of Brussels). In her weekly report to the authorities, Cavell said that she had directed the patients to the police as ordered – so if the patient didn't appear, he must have somehow become lost.

Cavell also became involved in a resistance group to help British, French and Belgian soldiers reach the Netherlands. She sheltered the soldiers at the hospital, and then one of the Belgian leaders of the organisation, Philippe Baucq, gave them money and a guide to the border. In this way she helped 200 soldiers, but the Germans became suspicious and planted two spies at the hospital: Monsieur Quien and his assistant Monsieur Jeannes. The spies soon realised that Cavell was hiding soldiers, and on 5 August 1915 Cavell was arrested, together with her second in command, Sister Elizabeth Wilkins. Wilkins was released, but Cavell wasn't, and on 7 August she was put in solitary confinement in the prison of St Gilles. She was permitted to write letters, so she wrote to Grace Jemmet and asked her to tell everyone 'I am quite all right here.' She asked for a red blanket, cutlery and crockery (ever practical, she added 'not best ones') and linen; she was concerned about her colleagues and her dogs.

Her nurses sent her flowers, and Cavell's letter of thanks for the flowers and letters reached Elizabeth Wilkins on 14 September. In typical Cavell fashion, she also told them to study hard and be on time for their classes.

She was court-martialled on 7 October along with eight others involved. The charge brought against her was 'having conspired to violate the German Military Penal Code' and 'conducting troops to the enemy', which equated to treason and the death sentence, though no written statement of her crime had been given to Cavell or her lawyer – and Cavell hadn't actually conducted the troops. She'd sheltered them.

Monsieur de Leval, the legal adviser to the American Legation, asked to be present at the trial, but the German military refused his request and told him that Mr Braun, a lawyer at the Brussels court, was defending her. Braun came to de Leval and said he couldn't defend her 'owing to unforeseen circumstances', but his friend Mr Kirschen would take his place. Kirschen confirmed this and told de Leval that the defence lawyers were not allowed to see their client before the trial or see any of the prosecution's documents. He also said it would be a long trial, as she was being prosecuted with 34 other prisoners, and he advised de Leval not to watch the trial, or the judge would take it that he was supervising the trial and it would prejudice Cavell's case. He also kept saying that the court was very fair, and he would do his best to defend Miss Cavell.

But the trial lasted for only two days, and the questions were asked in German (which Cavell did not speak) and passed on to her in French by a translator – and nobody could vouch that the translations were accurate.

At the trial Cavell admitted that she had helped the soldiers cross the frontier and go to England. When they asked her if she had helped 20, she said: 'More than twenty – two hundred.' She then admitted that they weren't all English – they were French and Belgian, too. One of the judges said she was foolish to help English soldiers, because they were ungrateful – Edith protested that was not true, because 'some of them have written from England to thank me'. Her response sealed her fate. When asked why she did it, she replied that if she hadn't the Germans would have shot them, and therefore she thought she was only

Stained glass window at Swardeston Church commemorating Edith Cavell. *(Photograph by author)*

doing her duty to her country in saving their lives. At the end of the trial, four of the resistance workers were sentenced to hard labour, and three had their executions adjourned; but Cavell and Baucq were to be executed immediately.

On 11 October Brand Whitlock, the American minister at Brussels, sent an appeal to Baron von der Lancken, head of the political department of the Governor-General of Belgium, and also to Baron von Bissing, the Governor-General. As well as appealing to their common humanity, Whitlock pointed out that Cavell was a nurse and had been of service to the Germans as well as the Allies; and also that she had confessed freely rather than lying.

Mr Gibson, the secretary of the American Legation, went with his legal adviser de Leval and the Spanish minister to see Baron von der Lancken and pleaded for Cavell to be spared. Von der Lancken first of all denied that the sentence had been passed, then said it was a matter for the military governor – who would not budge. Revd Stirling Gahan, the Anglican chaplain in Brussels, was allowed to see Cavell. She told him 'I thank God for this 10 weeks' quiet before the end...this time of rest has been a great mercy' – and then she said the words that will always be associated with her: 'But this I would say, standing as I do in view of God and eternity: I realise that patriotism is not enough. I must have no hatred or bitterness toward anyone.' They prayed together and recited the hymn *Abide With Me*. Cavell gave him a letter for her nurses to say goodbye and give them courage – and also to warn them against gossip:

> I have seen so much evil during these eight years that could have been avoided or lessened if there had not been a little word whispered here and there, perhaps not with bad intention – but it ruined the reputation and happiness, even the life of someone.

She added 'I have been perhaps too severe sometimes but never voluntarily unjust, and I have loved you all much more than you thought.'

She and Baucq were taken before two firing squads, who stood six paces away from her. Just before she was bound to the execution post, she told the German chaplain, Pastor Le Seur, 'Ask Mr Gahan to tell my loved ones later on that my soul, as I believe, is safe, and that I am glad to die for my country.'

Cavell was shot at dawn on 12 October 1915, and international uproar followed. Sir Edward Grey, the British Secretary of State for foreign affairs, said the execution should be viewed 'with horror and disgust not only in the Allied States, but throughout the civilised world'. As indeed it was; despite Germany saying it was justified in its actions, in just one day 10,000 new recruits enlisted in the army, and Cavell's execution was one of the reasons why the US entered the war in 1917. Dr Chilcote, the medical superintendent at St Pancras, said, 'She was an excellent night superintendent and an exceedingly nice woman. Although small and rather fragile, she was just the sort of woman who would help a fellow countryman at the risk of her life.'

Edith Cavell's funeral. *(Picture courtesy of Norfolk County Council Library and Information Service)*

Edith Cavell's grave on Life's Green. *(Photograph by author)*

On 20 October 1915 a memorial service was held for Cavell at St Paul's Cathedral. *The Times* reported that the 'churchyard was black with people, a great, silent, orderly crowd that waited and waited' and who had come there because 'they had been profoundly moved' by Edith Cavell. Queen Alexandra attended the service, and although there were seats for 600 nurses far more than that attended, all in uniform; the only colour was from the two scarlet ribbons tying their cloaks across their white aprons.

On 15 May 1919 Cavell's coffin was brought back from Dover to London, where King George V led a memorial service at Westminster Abbey. Then her body was taken through silent streets to Liverpool Street and was returned to Norwich by a special train. Her body was then taken to Norwich Cathedral, again through silent streets. Bishop Pollock described her as 'alive in God' and as someone who taught us that our patriotism must be examined in the light of something higher, then performed the last rites at her graveside in Life's Green.

SEVEN

Mary Chapman

Mary Ann Chapman.

Mary Ann Chapman was the founder of the first purpose-built mental hospital in the country; Bethel Street takes its name from the house she built there.

She was born on 24 March 1647, the fourth daughter of Dorothy Fountaine and John Mann. Her father was a tailor, described in the 1680s as 'the richest man in town'. John Mann was the sheriff and mayor of Norwich in 1649 and alderman in 1664, and he was also alderman and sheriff of London in 1669.

She married the Revd Samuel Chapman on 10 May 1682 – quite a late marriage, as she was 35 at the time, and he was 15 years older than she was. Samuel had been a widower for the past two years, and he was the rector of Drayton in 1669 and Thorpe St Andrew in 1670. He died on 29 June 1700 and was buried in the chancel of Thorpe St Andrew Church.

Not much is known about Chapman's life until about 1713, when she founded the Bethel hospital. She and Samuel both had relatives who had suffered from mental illness, and the Chapmans were horrified at the treatment meted out to the sick. As they had no children, Mary decided to build a hospital for the mentally ill and endowed it in her will. The wording of her will shows just how deeply she had been affected by seeing how the mentally ill were treated:

And whereas as it hath pleased Almighty God to visit and afflict some of my nearest relations and kindred with lunacy, but has hitherto blessed me with the use of my reason and understanding as a monument of my thankfulness unto God for this invaluable mercy and out of a deep sense of His divine goodness and undeserved love to me vouchsafed, and in compassion to the deplorable state of such persons as are deprived of their reason and understanding and are

The Bethel hospital, founded by Mary Chapman. *(Photograph by author)*

destitute of relations or friends to take care of them and also because it was much upon my good husband's thoughts to contribute something towards perpetual maintenance of this particular act of Charity, for all and every of these reasons by Will is that the House I have lately built in the Parish of Saint Peter's Mancroft...shall by my said Trustees...from time to time for ever after be used and employed for the convenient reception and habitation of poor lunaticks which it shall be called according to the desire of my said well beloved husband by the name of Bethel...

She settled 'all her estates in the county of Norfolk, or elsewhere' on seven trustees to fund the hospital, and she defined the 'poor lunatics' as those 'afflicted with lunacy or madness (not such as were fools or idiots from their birth)'. The plan was that the patients should be maintained, clothed and fed, and the trustees should manage it so as many people as possible could be kept there without having to pay. Citizens of Norwich were given preference for the places, but any deserving case in Norfolk would be considered.

However, she had clearly come across some kind of bad treatment of the mentally ill in an institution in the city (perhaps the Bridewell?), because her will also stated that:

...no trustee, or trustees, should resign or make over his or their trusts to the court of mayoralty of the said city, it being her express mind and will that this charity should never come into the hands of the said court, and that neither they, nor any of them, acting as a public society, should be in any way concerned in the execution of this trust.

Mary Chapman
1647~1724
Wife of the Reverend Samuel Chapman, founded this hospital known as Bethel in 1713, which was built wholly at her own expense.

Plaque on the front of the Bethel. *(Photograph by author)*

Originally Chapman lived in Thorpe and had a master running the hospital; but then she moved to the hospital, and it's thought that she played some part in nursing the sick.

She died on 8 January 1724, and the first board meeting of the trustees was held four days later. As she had requested, the word 'Bethel' (decided on by her 'well beloved' husband) was fixed over the front door, and under it the Biblical text from Hebrews xii. 16: 'But to do good and to communicate, forget not; for with such sacrifice God is well pleased.' The Bethel was made a public asylum in 1726, and by 1753 there were 28 patients there.

Chapman was buried next to her husband in the chancel of Thorpe St Andrew Church. The church fell into ruin for a time, and the inscription on her tomb was unreadable; however, towards the end of the 19th century a new marble stone was placed there at the expense of the Bethel hospital. The new wording read:

Under this stone resteth in hopes of a joyful resurrection the body of that exemplary pious and charitable widow Mrs MARY CHAPMAN, daughter of JOHN MAN [sic] esq., May or Norwich, and High Sheriff of Norfolk, and relict of the Rev. Mr, SAM. CHAPMAN, formerly rector of this church.

She built wholly at her own expence the house in Norwich called Bethel, for the reception, maintenance and care of poor lunaticks, to which and other charitable uses she gave all her income while she lived and her estate at her death, wch. happened on the 8th day of January in the year of our lord, 1724, and of her age the 76th.

'That this woman hath done shall be told for a memorial of her' Math. xxvi. 13.

There is also a green plaque to Mary Chapman on the front of the Bethel.

EIGHT

Jeremiah James Colman

The name of Jeremiah James Colman will always be thought of in connection with mustard – but he was far, far more than a businessman. He was probably the greatest philanthropist the city has ever known and regarded himself as his employees' friend and neighbour as well as their boss. He was a quiet giant who didn't like the showiness of municipal life and refused to lay foundation stones, on the grounds that he wouldn't lay them with enough dignity, and he believed in hard work. Even in his sixties, he got up at four in the morning to tend his gardens, worked through until 7.30pm, then went through the firm's accounts in the evening. He also believed that anything was possible and used to say, 'We don't use the word "can't" at Carrow.'

He was born on 14 June 1830 at Stoke Holy Cross; he joined the flour-milling and mustard-making business of his great-uncle Jeremiah Colman and his father James at the age of 17. The Colman family had a tradition of liberal nonconformism; the elder Jeremiah was the founder of the Lancastrian school in Norwich and started the Stoke Holy Cross New Benefit Society, and both he and James took the role of the sheriff and mayor of Norwich, so it was unsurprising that Colman followed in their footsteps. Colman was educated at Poringland in the company school, and then by a private tutor in Norwich.

In 1841 Jeremiah the elder moved to Norwich and left James in charge of the business at Stoke. When he died in 1851, J.J. Colman was brought into the partnership; then James died in 1854, leaving Colman in sole charge of the business at the age of 24. He was worried that running the family business plus its wealth and influence would cause him to be selfish and end up neglecting his faith, self-improvement and moral beliefs, but his mother reassured him that he'd be fine. And he most definitely lived up to her reassurances.

For a start, he realised that most of the firm's employees lived in Norwich and left home at 4.30am to be at the factory by 6, and they didn't get home until 7.30pm. So he thought that if he moved the firm to Norwich it would make their lives a lot easier by cutting down on travelling time. As well as being a caring employer, he was a shrewd businessman; he bought land belonging to the railway at Carrow which, because it was next to the railway line and the River Wensum, had excellent transport links.

Jeremiah James Colman. *(Picture courtesy of Norfolk County Council Library and Information Service)*

Between 1854 and 1862 he relocated the firm to newly built factories which would produce mustard, starch and laundry blue. The mustard mill opened at Carrow in 1856, and Colman brought in a new way of doing things to heighten appeal and sales. Before then, mustard powder went to grocers in large wooden casks; Colman introduced the idea of small decorated containers and bright yellow labels so that his product would be recognised on the shelves. The bull's head trademark was introduced in 1855 and was one of the first registered under the Trade Marks Act in 1875. He also changed the way flour was sold, bagging it individually rather than sending it to grocers in large sacks.

In 1866 Colman was appointed as the mustard maker to Queen Victoria. When he was asked to sum up the secret of his success and how he made a fortune out of such a humble thing as mustard, he replied, 'I make my money from the mustard that people throw away on the sides of their plate.' He was also awarded other royal warrants – by Napoleon III of France, the Prince of Wales and Victor Emmanuel II of Italy in 1869.

His products also won awards, including one for rice starch at the Crystal Palace exhibition in 1851, the only two grand gold medals at the 1872 Moscow Exhibition for mustard and his ultramarine starch 'Azure Blue' (a replacement for starch made from raw indigo), the only silver medal at the same exhibition for his cornflour, and the French Cross of the Legion of Honour in 1878.

Best of all, nothing went to waste at the mill: the husks of the mustard seeds were crushed and the oil extracted from them. The husks were made into cakes, sold as manure; and the oil was refined and used as a lubricant.

Colman wanted to lead a fulfilling but reverential business life. He decided to be useful, firstly by increasing employment opportunities in his home city, which had seen a slump in textile manufacturing (which he did through very successful marketing – increasing staff numbers from 1,100 in 1869 to 2,500 in 1898), and secondly by promoting the well-being of his employees. Before his marriage to his wife Caroline, he wrote to her:

I hope we shan't lead an ideal selfish existence, for I am sure that it won't be a happy one if we do. Influence, position and wealth are not given for nothing, and we must try and use them as we would wish at the last we had done.

To his relief, Caroline shared his beliefs and an article in *Commerce* magazine in 1893, called 'An East Anglian colony', said the Carrow employees were 'the most well-cared-for mass of operatives in the world'.

In 1857 he moved the company school to Carrow. At the time, education wasn't free; Colman paid the teachers, and the parents of the children paid 1d a week for the first child and ½d a week for subsequent children, which paid for school prizes. Colman wanted a wide curriculum to include reading, writing, spelling, maths, grammar, geography, history, drawing and scripture – though as always in his religion he believed in freedom of thought and insisted that 'nothing that bears the stamp of sect, party or denomination will intrude'. Caroline, being practical, added woodwork, domestic economy and Venetian ironwork to the curriculum. Colman's love of horticulture made him add gardening and beekeeping.

Although he and Caroline weren't teetotallers, they both felt that drink was responsible for many social ills, so Colman bought out the landlords of six out of the nine pubs within a quarter of a mile of Carrow and closed the pubs. However, he did build a coffee house at Trowse to give his employees a recreational facility. He also believed that all families should have land for growing flowers and vegetables, and he set aside some of his lands for allotments for the workers at Carrow.

A works kitchen opened in 1868 to give workers tea, coffee and hot midday meals cheaply. A meal of a quarter of a pound of meat, plus gravy and potatoes, cost just 3d – which covered the cost of the raw materials, and the company paid for the preparation and cooking costs. Caroline also set up lodging and laundry for young female workers, organised a clothing club (and she contributed a bonus to their savings), bought material in bulk and sold it to the workers at cost, and in 1874 she employed dressmaking teachers to help women to sew.

Colman insisted that all workers had to be insured against accidents and sickness, either through company schemes or through friendly societies. So the company dispensary, along with a doctor and nurse, opened in 1864. The company scheme meant that employees paid 1d a week, and if their wives or children were ill they had free medical attention. Colman appointed a sick visitor, too, to investigate cases of special need; and in 1878 32-year-old Philippa Flowerday was engaged as the first industrial nurse in the country, visiting sick employees with food from the works kitchen. Her duties included helping the doctor each morning in the dispensary then making 45 home visits per week in the afternoons.

The *Commerce* magazine article lists many of the employee benefits at Colman's, including a clothing club, a lending library, the dispensary, schools of cookery and technique, workmen's clubs, savings banks, refreshment rooms, reading rooms, playgrounds for the young, athletic grounds and '101 other good and noble helps to the healthy bringing-up'. Colman was also one of the first to introduce the idea of paid holidays for staff. He instituted an annual tea party on Whit Tuesday, but in

The Colman memorial in the Rosary Cemetery. *(Photograph by author)*

1877 there were too many employees to sit down, so he gave them a day's paid holiday instead. The office staff had a day off in September after the annual mustard delivery.

In 1896 Colman turned the firm into a limited liability company. But he put a clause in the articles of association so that charitable works to help sickness, infirmity and pension of the employees and families would continue after his death, and also in his will he left £20,000 annually for 20 years for trustees to use for this purpose.

As well as contributing hugely to the city's business community, Colman was involved in its religious and municipal life. He was a teaching member of St Mary's Baptist Chapel from 1850 and was deacon there from 1861–70. He was the city's sheriff in 1862 and the mayor in 1867, and he was the liberal MP for Norwich from 1871 to 1895 – so it is unsurprising that he was awarded the Freedom of the City in March 1893. He was a close personal friend of Gladstone but refused the prime minister's offer to ask Queen Victoria for a baronetcy. He helped to remove bribery and corruption from local government, and campaigned for franchise reform from 1859. In his obituary the local papers called him 'above all things an honourable and upright opponent'.

He also did much for the city's culture. He was one of the leaders of the subscription campaign to ensure the use of all historic buildings for the public benefit (by 1886 the castle and Blackfriars Hall were both owned by the corporation) and to preserve the city wall and towers. He was a trustee of Norwich Museum and bequeathed a large collection of paintings to them, including many of the Norwich School.

When he retired to the village of Carlton, near Lowestoft, he built a chapel, Sunday school, café and village hall. But 1895 brought two huge blows: Colman's son Alan died, aged only 28, shortly followed by his wife Caroline. Colman's way of dealing with it was to go back to work – and he also bought land for an extension to the Jenny Lind Children's Hospital to commemorate his son.

Colman caught the flu in February 1898, and although he recovered there was another set-back when his good friend William Gladstone died in May. His mother's death in September at the age of 93 was the final straw; Jeremiah Colman died three days later on 18 September 1898.

The *Norfolk Chronicle* reported:

> ...the city is deprived of a man who had ever been in the foremost ranks of those who have worked for its religious, social, charitable and commercial interests...freedom of religious thought and action was to him something more than a mere empty and meaningless phrase.

They added that although he had done much for the city, he had done even more in private: 'his deeds of private benevolence far outnumbered those acts of public liberality'. He had a quick mind and could see 'all the sides of a project at once and [eliminate] unnecessary detail'. And most importantly he had a reputation for strict integrity; farmers never bothered haggling with Colman about the price of corn because they knew he would be fair.

On the day of his funeral the windows of the city shops were shaded, and the bells of St Peter Mancroft rang a muffled peal. At the service in the Princes Street Chapel, the priest Dr Barrett said that Colman told him 'Money has its responsibilities as well as its privileges.' Colman certainly shouldered his responsibilities.

He was buried in the family plot in the Rosary cemetery. And the mayor of Norwich summed Colman up beautifully as 'a citizen whom [we] could not replace'.

NINE

John Sell Cotman

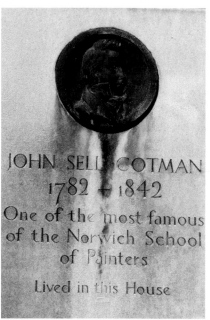

JOHN SELL COTMAN
1782 – 1842
One of the most famous
of the Norwich School
of Painters

Lived in this House

Plaque to John Sell Cotman, on his former house. *(Photograph by author)*

John Sell Cotman has been described as 'one of the world's greatest watercolourists' and 'one of the most original...most exquisitely gifted of the English landscape painters', but he was largely ignored during his lifetime, despite the fact he worked really hard. He was always a bit self-deprecating, and wrote to his patron Dawson Turner during the last year of his life:

> ...it was my play. For hard work I detest, and might – had I been put to it – been a sad idler...I know I have naturally many bad qualities – doing anything I dislike for one, keeping accounts for another.

Cotman was almost always short of money, partly because he was an inveterate collector of books and engravings, but in the early 20th century his work was recognised for its brilliance and at last he has his rightful place among the best artists of the UK.

The son of a hairdresser, Cotman was born on 16 May 1782 in the parish of St Mary Coslany in Norwich and baptised at St Mary Coslany Church. He always loved drawing and wrote to his patron Dawson Turner that his mother said he drew 'tips' (i.e. ships) long before he could speak.

By 3 August 1793 Cotman had a free place at Norwich Grammar School. His earliest known dated work is a pencil drawing of old houses in Mill Lane, Norwich, and his talent and love for drawing was so obvious that Cotman's father realised he didn't want to go into the family business. So he approached artist John Opie to talk about his son's future career

Cotman House, St Martin-at-Palace Plain. *(Photograph by author)*

in 1798. Opie's response was 'Let him rather black boots, than follow the profession of an artist.' In his lectures to students, Opie made it very clear that 'in no profession is the reward of his talents so precarious and uncertain'.

But Cotman wasn't deterred, and he went to study in London in 1798. He worked as an assistant to Rudolph Ackermann, a publisher of engravings and art dealer in the Strand, and he also became part of the London art set, meeting J.M.W. Turner and Thomas Girtin and joining Dr Thomas Monro's teaching 'academy'. (Monro was also a specialist in mental disorders – something that would play a large part in Cotman's life.)

In 1800, while he was living in Soho, Cotman had his first exhibition of watercolours at the Royal Academy, and the Society of Arts awarded him a large silver palette for his drawing of the mill at Dorking. The following year he was elected as a member of Girtin's Sketching Society, which had the aim of being a school of historic landscape. When Girtin died in 1802 the society became known as Cotman's Sketching Society.

Cotman visited Bristol and toured Wales twice – in common with most of the English landscape painters of the period – and also made three visits to Yorkshire, where he stayed at Brandsby Hall with the Cholmeleys and gave drawing lessons to the family. Mrs Cholmeley was the sister of Cotman's first patron, Sir Henry Englefield, and was very taken with him; she called him 'maniere'd and gentlemanlike' and wrote that he was 'quite a treasure – only 21 years old and such a draughtsman'. She also left him a bequest of £100 when she died in 1810. She was not the only one who appreciated Cotman, for his friendship with her son Francis Cholmeley was lifelong.

In his youth Cotman had quite a sense of humour; when one of his students sketched a well, he wrote 'well done' on the paper, and there are also many puns in his letters. One of the few stories about his childhood is the legend about his headmaster, Dr Forster, who didn't like cats. When Dr Forster discovered an incredibly lifelike black cat on his desk, cut out from cardboard, he knew exactly who had drawn it: his pupil who was the most talented artist, John Sell Cotman.

But then disappointment started to set in. In 1806 the Society of Painters in Water Colours (later known as the Old Watercolour Society) didn't elect him as a member, and Mrs Cholmeley wrote to her son in disgust that Cotman was blackballed by the Brook Street Society. This was probably because he had concentrated on his Yorkshire friends instead of developing influential friendships in London. In the same year Cotman held an exhibition at the Royal Academy and didn't sell much, so he decided to return to Norwich. He told Dawson Turner that he was going to turn himself about and study oil painting, which he had 'done but little, having been engaged too much in other things'.

Cotman set up a school of drawing in Luckett's Court off Wymer Street (now St Andrew's Street) and advertised in the *Norwich Mercury* on 1 July 1806 that he would give 'lessons in Painting and in Water Colours'. He also held a retrospective exhibition of his work, and he placed an advertisement in the *Norwich Mercury* on 20 December 1806 stating that he would open the exhibition and then the drawing school. He repeated the advertisement on 27 December, saying there would be over 400 drawings. Another advertisement of 10 January 1807 told would-be students that Cotman would start teaching on Monday 19 January 1807; the terms were £2 2s 0d quarterly in the Academy, or four private lessons for £1 1s 0d.

He started working in oils and liked the medium so much that he wrote to James Bulwer, 'I have been, and am, painting hard, and I am so fond of it that I think I shall never execute another drawing.' He was a major exhibitor with the Norwich Society of Artists in 1807; between 1807 and 1810 he showed 149 works, and also advertised himself as a portrait painter in their catalogue of 1808.

In 1809 Cotman married Ann Miles in Felbrigg Church. Clearly he loved her dearly; he used to call her his 'dear Nance' and wrote to her in 1817 as 'My Love, My Wife, My everything.'

On 22 July 1809 Cotman advertised his 'circulating library' in the *Norfolk Chronicle*. The library consisted of 600 numbered drawings for pupils to copy. This was the same system as Ackermann had used in London, but it was new to Norwich and gave him an advantage over the other local drawing masters. A quarterly subscription to his library cost 1 guinea, and he delivered the pictures to subscribers himself on Mondays and Thursdays between 12 and 2.

In 1810 Cotman sent four oil paintings to the British Institution in Pall Mall and drawings to 'The Associated Painters in Water Colours' in Old Bond Street, but again his work didn't sell as it wasn't to the public's taste (and even now, nearly 200 years later, his work looks fresh and modern – it must have been a real shock to his contemporaries). It would be 15 years before he sent anything to London again. Later that year he became vice-president of the Norwich Society of Artists, although he didn't sell anything there either. But one bright spot in the year was the birth of his first son, Miles.

The following year Cotman published *Miscellaneous Etchings*, 26 landscape and architecture views of England and Wales. He thought he would be more successful and told Francis Cholmeley, 'I feel I have a horse that will carry me nearer the temple of fame than ever I was.' That same year he told Dawson Turner that he planned to 'commence Etchings of all Ornamented Antiquities in Norfolk'. But sadly his finances failed again.

In April 1812 the Cotman family moved to Yarmouth, and Cotman became the drawing tutor to Dawson Turner's daughters and wife for two days per week at a salary of £200 a year (the equivalent of just over £9,000 nowadays). However, he apparently wasn't that keen on teaching; he said to Dawson Turner, 'Saving for the best scholars it's but a sorry drudgery and only calculated for money-making when a man fags from door to door merely for the pound sterling.' His daughter Ann was born, and to make more money Cotman became an archaeological draughtsman; however, he worked so hard that it affected his eyesight. He spent 1813 very ill with what his biographer Sydney Kitson called a 'brain storm' – fever and depression – and the following year he had to have an operation on his eyes. At that point he needed to employ apprentices to make his etchings. His family was also growing; John Joseph was born in 1814, Francis Walter was born in 1816 and Alfred was born in December 1817 (but sadly died).

In 1817 he undertook the first of three tours of Normandy (the second being in 1818 and the third in 1820). He received a camera lucida from his patron Sir Henry Englefield and used it a lot in Normandy, especially for capturing the detail of church buildings. He wrote to Francis Cholmeley in 1817 that he 'only finished the works and sketches abroad' because of the problems with his eyes. But although his paintings of the period were brilliant, he didn't exhibit them until 1825 – and by then he had missed the bandwagon as the public's desire for etchings from Normandy was already sated.

In October 1819 the Cotmans had another son, also called Alfred, and Cotman published his engravings of sepulchral brasses of Norfolk and Suffolk. He was incredibly busy over the next three years at Yarmouth and wrote to Francis Cholmeley in 1822 that he worked from 8.30am until dusk, with one hour's break for dinner, winter or summer.

Cotman went to London in June 1822 and became ill; he claimed his illness was caused by 'inadvertently swallowing a bone', but it grew worse when he returned home, and he had a nervous breakdown. He was seriously ill with a liver complaint in 1823, followed by great unhappiness when his daughter Mary was born and died only two months later.

Yet again, Cotman threw himself into work. In summer 1823 he exhibited 19 works with the Norwich Society, his first large exhibition with them since he went to live in Yarmouth. The *Norwich Mercury* was complimentary: 'He is a man of uncommon powers, both intellectual and practical...a style of his own...talent which sets him above the level of common faculties.' Cotman decided to come back to Norwich and opened a school of drawing in a house at St Martin-at-Palace.

He sold most of his work from his years in Yarmouth at an auction at Christie's in London on 1 May 1824 to finance the house, but he was disappointed by the results after altogether raising only £165 6s 4d for 250 drawings, an average of 12 shillings and sixpence each (the equivalent of just £42 in modern terms).

In 1825 Cotman finally became an associate of the Society of Painters in Water Colours (also known as the Old Watercolour Society) but was never to become a full member. He was still suffering from depressive illness – an illness which his sons John Joseph and Alfred also shared – and he still wasn't earning as much as he had hoped. He'd had enough and wanted to go back to London. He wrote to Mrs Dawson Turner in March 1825, 'London, with all its fog and smoke, is the only air for an artist to breathe in'. But he was doomed to disappointment again; although he applied for the post of drawing master at the School of Military Engineering in Chatham, he wasn't accepted. Then Robert Hunt at *The Examiner* criticised his works at the Old Watercolour Society for their 'sudden opposition of reds, blues and yellows'. Cotman fell back into depression and wrote in August 1826, 'the sun has set for ever on my career and all is darkness before me'. He was also worried that because he'd lost so many pupils he would have to go to the workhouse.

By 1827 things started to get better and he had more pupils on his books, but he lapsed into depression again in 1829. During 1831–2 he was vice-president of the Norwich Society of Artists; he became president in 1833 but disbanded the society the same year.

In 1834 he was longing to return to London. Samuel Bignold wrote a glowing reference about Cotman's ability to teach drawing and his 'habits and character', and Cotman became Professor of Drawing at King's College. He celebrated his appointment by sending a new dress to his wife and another to his daughter, and he wrote to his wife: 'Much as I have ever loved London I have never trod its gold paved streets feeling so much a man of business, and so much to belong to it, as now.'

He spent the next year living in Bloomsbury, trying to get enough money together to obtain a house big enough for his family; clearly he was miserable, as he wrote to Dawson Turner that 'the income is not sufficient' and 'a lodging is no home: a divided family is no blessing'. Dawson Turner refused to give him a loan, but pointed out that Cotman was an avid collector and had a very valuable collection of paintings and books which could be sold to help him. (Even though he had financial worries, Cotman was still collecting prints and books in London; he wrote to his son John Joseph that he had 'added most wonderfully' to his library and claimed his purchases were 'very cheap' – as anyone with a rare book collector in their family will attest, they were far from cheap!)

So Cotman held yet another auction. Personally, it wasn't a success for him – his own paintings sold very cheaply, and he put an unrealisable reserve of 600 guineas on the copper plates of his etchings. But the sale raised £500, and he settled his debts, which were less than he thought, and finally his family joined him in London. At the end of the year he wrote to Dawson Turner, 'I feel now perfectly happy…my wretched feelings have all left me.' He also thought of his old rival and friend John Crome's family, who were struggling to make a living, and he asked Dawson Turner to help them.

London suited Cotman. He only had to attend classes on Wednesday and Saturday, and he provided drawing copies for his pupils (aided by Miles, his eldest son). He wanted his pupils to love and respect his drawings and in that he was successful, because his pupil Sarah Stickney wrote in her book *The Poetry Of Life* that Cotman was 'one of the most poetical artists of the present day'. D.G. Rossetti and his younger brother William were also pupils; William Rossetti described Cotman as 'an alert, forceful-looking man, of modest stature, with a fine well-moulded face, which testified to an impulsive nature, somewhat worn and worried'.

The worries were due to his family life; Miles was ill, John Joseph suffered from depression and Alfred was unstable. John Joseph had remained in Norwich, and one letter from Cotman tells him what to charge as a minimum for lessons: 'You gain no credit by working under price; if a man doesn't value himself he will be undervalued by the world, depend on it.' But John Joseph became ill again, and in 1837 had to be placed in care 'to keep quiet and contented'. He recovered his health and returned to Norwich, but the drawing school failed and he was in debt. Cotman told him to come to London, where he would give him four hours work a day, but his son refused to leave Norwich. Cotman wrote to him with more advice: 'draw sternly and true...Leave out, but add nothing'.

By 1839 Cotman was depressed again. In 1841 he embarked on a last sketching tour in Norfolk; he visited his friend James Bulwer, his father and his patron Dawson Turner. He wrote to Dawson Turner about sketching on Mousehold Heath; he was late for dinner with his father, and had to gallop through a hailstorm, but couldn't resist stopping to sketch 'a magnificent scene on the top of the hill leading down to Col Harvey's house, of trees and gravel pit. But Norfolk is full of such scene. Oh! rare and beautiful Norfolk'.

After the relief of Norfolk, Cotman returned to London. He was in denial about his son Alfred's insanity, but he told Dawson Turner that he was having problems and Alfred had caused 'dangerous and distressing scenes'.

In July 1842 Cotman was ill again. He wouldn't eat or sleep, and his daughter Ann told John Joseph 'I am quite sure he does not wish to get well, or he would have made some effort to do so'. Cotman died in Bloomsbury on 24 July 1842 'of natural decay' and was buried in St John's Wood Chapel Churchyard, Marylebone.

After his death an auction of his work was held, which raised just over £200. Another auction also had poor results – but there was one huge benefit for Norwich. James Reeve, the curator of the Castle Museum, collected Cotman's paintings and exhibited 100 watercolours and 100 drawings there in July 1888. He sold half of his collection to the museum in 1902, and the other half to Sir Henry Theobald, who later went blind and sold them to Russell Colman – who in turn left them to the Castle Museum.

Although Cotman was unappreciated during his lifetime and died in obscurity – the great Victorian art critic John Ruskin doesn't even mention him – in the late Victorian era his beautiful watercolours and etchings finally started to gain the respect they deserved, and now Cotman finally has his place as one of the finest Romantic landscape artists.

TEN

William Crotch

William Crotch. *(Photograph by kind permission of Norwich Castle Museum and Art Gallery)*

William Crotch was Norwich's answer to Mozart: a musical child prodigy who played for the King of England when he was little more than a toddler and who toured the country, playing to crowds.

Crotch was born in Green's Lane in St George's Colegate parish on 5 July 1775, the son of carpenter Michael Crotch and his second wife Isabella. He had two older half-brothers, Michael and John. His father built an organ and used to play *God Save the King* on it; at the age of 18 months Crotch loved music and would even leave his dinner to listen. He used to toddle over to the organ and touch the first note of his favourite tunes to get his father to play them; if his father didn't play them straight away, the toddler would play the next couple of notes too.

When Crotch was just two years and three weeks old, his father was visited by a friend, Mrs Lulman, who played the organ and sang her own accompaniment. That night, when Crotch was being carried to bed, he screamed to go to the organ and tried to play it. The following day he persuaded his 14-year-old half-brother John to blow the bellows and started to play the organ himself. He played *God Save the King* – amazing his father, who was working in the garret. The next day he added the treble, and the following day he added the bass except for one note that was an octave below, and he couldn't quite reach it.

His parents tried to keep his abilities quiet, because they thought nobody would believe them, but word spread. One day Michael Crotch was off sick when his employer, the weaver Mr Paul, passed the house and heard the organ playing. Thinking that Michael was skiving, he stormed into the house, ready to give the carpenter a piece of his mind, and discovered little William Crotch sitting on his brother's knee, playing the organ. He rushed out and told neighbours, bringing them in to the house to prove that the baby was playing the music. The following day people besieged the house to hear young Crotch play.

Charles Burney (a musical historian and friend of George III) also heard Crotch play and reported it in *Gentleman's Magazine*, claiming 'at present he plays nothing correctly, and his voluntaries are little less wild than the native notes of a lark or a black-bird', but Burney also added that Crotch didn't look at the keys when he played, could only stretch to a sixth and used his knuckles to play fast passages.

Crotch's mother took him on tour when he was only three. His first recitals were at Ipswich, Oxford, Framlingham and Bury. In October 1778 Crotch started playing in London. He was introduced to J.C. Bach, who arranged for him to play before George III on 1 January 1779 – and the king was highly impressed by the young prodigy. Some accounts claim that George III was playing *God Save the King* and introduced some wrong notes, and young Crotch pushed him aside crying, 'That's not right, you fool!' There may be some truth in this as he used to get angry and tell people how to play if they played wrong notes, and in later life Crotch admitted that he was a spoilt child, 'petted, flattered and encouraged to be rude'.

For the next four years Crotch continued to tour with his mother and taught himself to play the violin – though he held the instrument as if it were a cello. He said later that he remembered these tours with pain and humiliation, particularly 'the manner in which my uncultivated abilities had been displayed to audiences who were frequently as ignorant of what was good and correct as myself'.

In April 1786 Crotch moved to Cambridge and became assistant to Dr John Randall, the professor of music. Crotch's oratorio, *The Captivity of Judah*, was played at Trinity Hall, Cambridge, when he was still only 14. He composed the chime for the new clock at Great St Mary's Church of London in 1793; the chime was used in the clock tower in the Houses of Parliament from 1859 and became known as the Westminster chimes. Although he intended to make his career in the church, he went to Oxford in 1788 and ended up studying music. He was also gifted at art and used to inscribe drawings with the precise time they were made as well as the date.

In 1790 he was appointed the organist of Christ Church Cathedral and was awarded his degree in music four years later. He married Martha Bliss in July 1797, at the age of 22; he said he had 'admired her for nine, loved her for seven and courted her for five years'. The family moved to Broad Street, and Crotch built an observatory on the roof of their house. The same year he was appointed professor of music at Oxford. One of his duties as professor was to judge the musical compositions submitted as exercises; he had to judge his own compositions (which seems very wrong to modern eyes, but was protocol in its day) and received his doctorate in 1799.

Crotch had a strong business acumen and earnt huge amounts. He became a lecturer on music to the Royal Institution in the early 1800s and moved to London in 1805. He was also the music director of the Birmingham festival, but clashed with the organisers and wasn't invited back. He charged a fee of £540 in 1810 (equivalent to just over £28,000 today) for directing a four-day festival in Oxford when Lord Greville became chancellor of the university. He wrote the oratorio *Palestine* but didn't publish it and would only let it be performed if he was the director (at a fee of £200 in 1812 – the equivalent of just over £9,000 in today's money). Samuel Wesley said in a letter to Vincent Novello that Crotch 'loves Money better than real Reputation'.

In 1822 Lord Burghersh invited Crotch to be the first principal of the Royal Academy of Music in London. The idea was that he would be responsible for administration, teaching harmony and counterpoint, and organising concerts. However, Crotch kept clashing with Burghersh; Burghersh wanted his own operas staged, but Crotch didn't think they were good enough so kept refusing to stage them. In December 1831, when Crotch was caught kissing a female student (which he claimed was to say well done for working on a harmony exercise), he was forced to resign from the academy.

Crotch more or less retired from music at this point, especially as three of his four surviving children died in the period just before and just after his resignation. He judged some prizes (including the Gresham Prize in 1832) but was attacked for having conservative views on music. He said that Mozart was 'the greatest of all modern composers' after hearing the *Requiem*, and Beethoven's piano music was 'original and masterly, frequently sublime';

however, Crotch didn't like Beethoven's symphonies at all, saying that he disregarded the rules of composition.

During his last years Crotch was in poor health. He had much trouble with his knees and ankles, which confined him to bed, and he also suffered from aches in his shoulder, recurring nosebleeds and chest pains. He and his wife went to live with their son William in Taunton, and Crotch died from a heart attack in the middle of a meal on 29 December 1847. Somewhat gruesomely, he remained sitting upright at the table even after his death.

Although Crotch himself is practically forgotten nowadays, his music lives on and the Westminster chimes are a reminder of the Norwich toddler who once played for the king.

ELEVEN

John Fransham

'Horn-buttoned Jack' was probably one of the city's greatest eccentrics, and he was even lampooned on the London stage. Though if it wasn't for a memoir written by his former pupil William Saint, the master in mathematics at the Royal Military Academy in Woolwich, his character would have been lost to history.

John Fransham was baptised on 19 March 1730 in the parish of St George of Colgate, Norwich, the first of the two children of Thomas Fransham, the parish sexton, and his wife Isidora. Fransham was taught Latin and theology, but because his parents were poor he had to go out to work. He was apprenticed to a cooper at Wymondham but loathed the job and deserted his master within three weeks. His father, exasperated, told Fransham that he couldn't afford to keep him in shoes, and Fransham's immediate reaction was to stop wearing shoes and stockings – and he kept this up for three years.

His parents, worried about his eccentric behaviour, contacted the noted city doctor Sir Benjamin Wrench. Fransham had just received a legacy of £25 and planned to buy a horse; Wrench said he would offer Fransham a horse, sight unseen, for £30 and see what his reaction was. According to Saint, Fransham realised his parents were testing him, so he decided to tease Wrench by claiming that he wouldn't ride the horse but would make a friend of it and lead it about. Wrench fell for it, and Fransham listened in glee at the door as Wrench told Thomas Fransham, 'You must keep him low and by no means contradict him.' Fransham thoroughly enjoyed repeating the story to his students.

Fransham wanted to study maths and discovered he was very good at it, but his parents needed him to work and contribute to the household income, so they persuaded him to become an amanuensis for an attorney, Mr Marshall. Fransham quickly grew bored and went to learn weaving from Daniel Wright. He stuck at the job for the next two years, until Wright's death.

In 1748 Fransham left home, walked to Great Yarmouth and took a boat to South Shields with the intention of touring the Highlands. He became friendly with some soldiers and enlisted in the army at Newcastle, but he was discharged because he had bandy legs. He managed to get back from Newcastle to Norwich with 3½d and a Scotch plaid – all that was left of his possessions.

His next job was as an actor. He joined a company of strolling players (and played Iago and Shylock), but the audiences were small and the manager paid the players in turnips. Fransham didn't mind until he found out that the turnips were stolen; then he left the troupe in disgust to become a tutor to Hellesdon farmer Barnaby Leman's children for a couple of years, before returning to his job as an amanuensis.

Fransham became a member of a society in Norwich for 'men of original minds and small incomes', where he met the farrier Mr Clover. He came to an arrangement with Clover whereby he taught the farrier Latin and classics, while Clover taught him maths. He was still very fond of animals and asked if he could lead home the horses Clover had shod so they wouldn't suffer by being ridden too soon after shoeing. Clover's workmen weren't happy about this and showed their displeasure by throwing hot horseshoes around the shop. Because Fransham didn't wear shoes, his feet obviously tended to get burned, so he was forced to choose between wearing shoes again or giving up the care of horses. His humanitarian side won and he chose to wear shoes. He was firmly against the

View of the city from Mousehold Heath.*(Photograph by author)*

practice of docking horses' tails and 'nicking' (making a cut under the horse's tail so it would hold its tail higher), and when asked who he would vote for, he replied: 'Him who has humanity enough to drive long-tailed horses.'

Between 1760 and 1771 Fransham worked as an amanuensis and tutor. His sister worked as the housekeeper to the Chute family, and she put in a good word for him so they allowed him to sleep there and use the library. But then Fransham had a fey episode; he dreamt that he heard young Mr Chute call to him twice. Fransham dressed and went downstairs to meet him, but nobody was there. He went back to bed and told his sister about his dream the next morning; as Chute had been lying ill at Pickenham, she thought it was a presage of his death. A few hours later they heard the news that Chute was dead.

At this point Fransham was patronless and penniless, having little business from the attorneys and no pupils. So he bought a farthing's worth of potatoes every day and lived on just potatoes and salt. Then he thought he would try sleeping outside, in case his poverty got worse; he spent one night on Mousehold Heath with turf as a pillow and his Scotch plaid as a cover, but he caught a bad cold and didn't repeat the experiment.

The Quaker Samuel Leeds travelled from Norwich to London to be a physician. He had to go to the College of Physicians to be examined about his knowledge and skill in medicine, so he sent for Fransham to come and tutor him to improve his Latin, at terms of 1 guinea a week. Fransham spent nine months in London, but then Leeds's practice declined and he died. Fransham said that Leeds had died from a broken heart because of the unkind treatment meted out to him. Fransham then set up a booth at Hyde Park Corner; he also wrote papers on philosophy, but they were never published, so he had to go back to teaching to earn a living. He lost the sight of one eye temporarily, but when the weather turned from warm to cold his sight returned.

During this period the playwright Samuel Foote satirised him as 'Johnny Macpherson' in *The Devil upon Two Sticks*, portraying him as quarrelsome, naïve and boasting of his 'three-pence an hour for larning Latin to a physician in the ceety'.

1771 saw Fransham back in Norwich. He taught the children of the Cooper family at Brooke. He used to walk there on Saturday and return to Norwich on Monday, but after two years the distance became too much for him, and he was forced to give up. He wasn't paid for his tuition, just given his board and lodgings; but when Dr Cooper moved to a profitable practice at Great

Yarmouth, Fransham asked his friend Mr Robinson if he thought it was worth asking Dr Cooper to pay him a guinea for those two years. When Robinson suggested writing to him, Fransham said he didn't know how to write or fold a letter (even though he'd written several volumes of philosophy and Socratic dialogues, he'd never written a letter), so Robinson helped him. There was no reply, so Fransham decided never to write another letter – but then Cooper wrote back apologising for the delay because he had been away, thanked him for his work and sent him £5.

Fransham set up a school for classics and maths. Lessons were held between 6 and 8am in summer and 6 and 8pm in the winter. He had around 15 or 20 pupils, and charged them a shilling a week. He trusted the children to bring the money but, when some of them absconded and spent their lesson money on sweets, he changed the terms of his fees to a quarterly payment of half a guinea.

He was a keen collector of books, but was always scrupulous about paying the proper price and not getting a bargain. At one point, according to William Saint, he bought a small book for 2 shillings from 'the book-stall of some old woman'. When a friend told him the book was rare and worth 7 shillings, Fransham returned to the book-stall and insisted on paying 5 shillings more to the stallholder.

In 1784 Fransham went to live with his friend Mr Robinson. He continued running his school and spent his free time talking to Robinson about philosophy. His eccentricities really came to the fore from here; he'd taken up playing the drums for exercise, but when a neighbour complained about the noise, Fransham played a cane chair as a drum instead. He also played the hautboy until one day, when he had a headache, he couldn't find fuel to make a pot of tea, so he burned the hautboy for fuel.

He then took up the 'bilbo-catch' or 'bilver-ketch' (a toy with a ball attached to a cup on a spiked end – Fransham naturally insisted on doing it the difficult way and catching the ball on the spiked end rather than in the cup) and practised until he could catch the ball 200 times in succession without missing. If a pupil wasn't ready for him, Fransham would take out the toy and wouldn't pay any attention to the pupil until he had caught the ball 200 times.

In 1785 Robinson's nephew developed consumption. Robinson went to see how he was, and on his return Fransham met him and said, 'I find you have lost your nephew' – in a similar dream to the one he'd had about Chute, Fransham had dreamed that the nephew had called him by name. And Robinson's nephew had indeed died.

His appearance grew even more eccentric after this. He was called 'horn-buttoned Jack' by his schoolboys, because he wore a short green jacket with large horn buttons, along with a huge hat, large shoes and short worsted stockings. He also wore his grey hair loose about his shoulders. In hot weather he used to carry his jacket on his arm and his hat in his hand. One day he met a Quaker who said he looked cool and comfortable. Fransham replied that the Quaker looked hot and uncomfortable, because he didn't have enough courage to follow Fransham's example. The Quaker was horrified, saying that decency forbade it and 'I like to have some regard to decency'.

In Fransham's philosophy he always turned evils into blessings. At one point he had managed to save £100 and his friends urged him to put it in the bank for safekeeping. Fransham quoted Virgil to them: '*Non bene ripae creditor.*' (In other words, 'it isn't safe to trust the bank'.) But he gave in and deposited the money with a merchant. He withdrew £75 of the money a couple of weeks before the merchant became bankrupt and, although he had still lost £25, he took the view that he had actually saved £75.

Fransham was terribly afraid of fire and, because Robinson's groom was careless, Fransham was convinced he would set light to the stable with a candle. So he kept a ladder in his bedroom to help him escape if necessary, and he practised running up and down it with a box that would contain his manuscripts. He used to practise every day at midday, and crowds used to gather to watch him. Then it occurred to him that if the fire erupted at night, he slept so soundly that he might not wake in time to escape. So he left Robinson's house and took a room in the parish of St Michael's at Plea until the stable was converted to another use; then he returned to stay with Robinson until his friend moved to a smaller house with no room for guests.

Playing with his bilbo-catch was still a hobby of Fransham's; his aim was to catch it 666,666 times, and he had a system of moving nuts in his pocket to a box to calculate how many times he had thrown it. He believed that health could only be appreciated if you were sick, so every so often he went to the confectioner's shop and ate so many cakes that he gave himself a headache, then cured himself with tea and reminded himself how valuable his health was. But generally he was abstemious, rising at 5am in the summer and 6am in winter. He rarely ate meat and didn't drink alcohol. His main diet was bread, butter and tea, and he was known to throw butter into the fire when it was bad; when a relative suggested giving it away rather than burning it, he refused because he couldn't offer something to a fellow creature that he couldn't eat himself.

In 1800 he went to live with Mr Jay the baker in St Clement's. He talked a lot to Mrs Jay about philosophy (the baker wasn't interested), and he wouldn't let her make his bed more than once a week because he said it was idle luxury. He also refused to let her wash his floor or whitewash his walls, as he was worried about damp.

Fransham didn't like dogs because he thought they were 'noisy, mobbish and vulgar', and if he went into a room inhabited by a dog, he asked the owner if the dog could retire. In his philosophical tract *'Aristopeia*, or ideal state', he said that all

St George's Church, Colegate.
(Photograph by author)

dogs would be exterminated. He also disliked young children, as he thought they interrupted conversation, disturbed quiet and frequently offended against manners and decency. However, he did like cats.

In 1805 his relative Mrs Smith was in distressed circumstances, so he hired a chamber and garret in St George's Colegate next to the wool hall and employed her as his housekeeper. He would have preferred to live in the garret himself, but he didn't want his pupils to disturb her as they went to and fro. When she found a better situation, he moved to a garret in Elm Hill, saying: 'A garret is the quietest room in the house; there are no rude noises overhead; all is calm and serene; nothing is to be heard, but the delightful "music of the rolling spheres".'

At the end of 1809 Fransham developed a severe cough and by January 1810 he was too feeble to take exercise. On 1 February he said to his nurse that he was worried about being buried alive. He asked her to move him from his bed to a chair and said if she thought he was motionless she should shake him well. If that didn't work, she should place him by a large fire 'within the scent of a hot apple-pye', and if that didn't work, she should put a beautiful woman by his side – and if that failed, she could consider him dead. A few minutes later she realised that she hadn't heard him cough for a while and discovered that he had died, sitting next to the fire.

He was buried at St George's Church in Colegate.

TWELVE

Elizabeth Fry

Elizabeth Fry is renowned throughout the country for her work with prisons, but she was originally Betsy Gurney, a Norwich Quaker who loved bright clothing and – ironically, as most of her work involved them – was frightened of dark places and the sea.

She was born into a family of wealthy Quaker bankers on 21 May 1780, the fourth of the 12 Gurney children, and well loved by her family; her mother Catherine called her 'my dove-like Betsy'. Fry was taught at home and learnt history, geography, French and Latin. Owing to ill health, she missed many lessons, and she also tended not to pay attention to tutors, so she was

Elizabeth Fry.

hopeless at spelling and felt very inferior to her sisters Catherine and Rachel. But she was heavily influenced by her mother, who visited the sick and the poor.

By 1798 the Gurney family took view that religion was something to be looked down on. They wore bright colours (Fry delighted in wearing a scarlet cloak and purple boots with red laces) and didn't go to regular Quaker meetings. Fry read the works of Paine and Rousseau and discussed them with her family. For a while she became a republican and used to ride through Norwich with a tricolour in her

Plaque to Elizabeth Fry near her birthplace – Gurney Court, off Magdalen Street. *(Photograph by author)*

hat. However, Fry underwent a religious conversion. The travelling Quaker William Savery visited Norwich in February 1798 to preach, and she wrote in her diary, 'Today I felt that there is a God. I have longed for virtue. I hope to be truly virtuous.' She asked to go to London and her father agreed, thinking that it might cheer her up. She went to the theatre, balls, operas and dinners, but she felt that something was missing. Then she heard Savery preach again in Westminster and became a strict Quaker. In 1799 she adopted plain Quaker dress and speech (calling everyone 'thee' and 'thou' instead of making the contemporary distinction calling the upper classes 'you'), and people in Norwich stopped inviting her to social events because they thought her religion was more important to her.

Mr Gurney took his family on a tour of England and Wales, staying with wealthy Quaker friends. An elderly friend of the family, Deborah Darby, said she thought Elizabeth Gurney would become 'a light to the blind, speech to the dumb and feet to the lame'. And how prophetic she was.

Fry set up a Sunday school in Earlham, to teach the children who worked in Norwich factories to read and write. She read them Bible stories, and her sisters called them 'Betsy's Imps'. Her school grew so large that she had to use the laundry room to teach them.

In 1799 she met London merchant Joseph Fry. She thought him shy and dull and refused his offer of marriage, but fell in love with him. One story is that he left a gold watch on a bench and if she picked it up, she would marry him, and if she left it, she wouldn't. Her sisters saw her go to the bench, look at the watch, think about it, walk away, come back, hesitate and finally pick up the watch. Fry's family didn't think she was enough of a plain Quaker, and Fry himself told her that her manners 'had too

Earlham Hall, where Elizabeth Fry grew up. *(Photograph courtesy of the University of East Anglia)*

much the courtier about them' – but she realised that he was a strong enough character to support her work outside the home. In 1800 she married Joseph in the Friends' Meeting House in Goat Lane then moved to London with him.

She had 10 children between 1801 and 1816 and an 11th child in 1822. She wrote in her diary that she was worried about becoming 'the careworn and oppressed mother' and started visiting Islington Workhouse to teach the children there. The Society of Friends acknowledged her as a minister in 1811, but by 1812 Fry was confiding to her diary that 'I fear that my life is slipping away to little purpose'. Then she met the exiled French aristocrat Stephen Grellet, a Quaker who had visited Newgate prison and had been horrified to see women lying on bare stone floors and newborn babies with no clothes. He asked Elizabeth to help; she immediately bought material and asked other Quakers to help make clothes for the children.

In 1813 she visited Newgate with her sister-in-law Anna Buxton. The turnkey refused to let her in at first, as he said the prisoners were 'savage', but Fry insisted. She was appalled to see women taking clothes off a dead baby to give to another child, so she gave out the clothes she had made and collected. On her second visit she brought more clothes, as well as clean straw for the women to lie on, and on her next visit she prayed for them. She was shocked by the conditions they were living in: 300 people were crowded into two rooms regardless of their gender, age, whether they had been tried or were still waiting to go to court, or whether they were a first offender or a hardened criminal. Her belief was that they were all fellow human beings whose treatment should be based on 'the principles of justice and humanity'. Fry claimed that if you wanted to 'amend the Character and change the Heart', you must treat prisoners with kindness instead of cruelty and neglect. She believed that prison should be for reform, not just punishment.

Fry wrote a report recommending the separation of male and female prisoners, classification of criminals, having female supervision for female prisoners and providing education and useful employment for prisoners – but she was unable to follow it through because family life took over. Her husband's business was in financial trouble after the economic slump following the Napoleonic war, she had two more children and her four-year-old daughter Betsy died.

But in late 1816 she was able to return to Newgate. She saw women fighting but was unafraid and simply picked up a child and asked, 'Is there not something we can do for these innocent little children?' She suggested setting up a school, and when she returned to give the first lesson, the female prisoners had tried to clean the prison and were ready to help.

Her brothers-in-law didn't think her plans would work and refused to give her backing. Fry wasn't deterred in the slightest. She set up a committee of 11 Quaker women and a clergyman's wife, and her husband helped her set up a meeting with the prison governor. She established a school for the children of the prisoners at Newgate, and the prisoners chose Mary Connor to act as schoolmistress. (Mary always said she was innocent of any crime; she was given a free pardon 15 months later, but sadly she had caught tuberculosis in Newgate and died.) Fry also worked with others to talk to prisoners, meet prison governors and establish changes.

In April 1817 Fry set up the Ladies' Association for the Reformation of the Female Prisoners in Newgate, starting with the prisoners who had already been tried; she suggested that there should be a specific prison dress, the prisoners should be classified, there should be a matron and monitors, the prisoners should have religious and elementary education and there should be paid employment. She began by putting the prisoners into groups of 12 with a monitor in each group (chosen by the prisoners themselves) who could read, plus a matron of their choice to superintend them. The day was structured so that at 9am they would hear a Scripture reading, then go to do knitting and needlework, then hand their work in to the matron at 6pm and hear another Scripture reading.

The prisoners at Newgate had always been regarded as the worst of the worst, but the changes in their behaviour, thanks to Fry's system, showed the prison governors that prisoners could be reformed. Although not all of the prisoners were happy about the removal of alcohol and cards, it meant that conditions changed greatly for the better. Fry visited Newgate or sent one of her helpers there every day, and she read the Bible to the prisoners herself on Fridays. The Mayor of London heard that conditions in the prison had changed and went to see for himself. He heard her read to the prisoners and was so impressed by the changes that he agreed to pay part of the matron's wages. The system worked so well that those who were in prison awaiting trial were also allowed to take part.

On 27 February 1818 Fry was the first woman to give evidence to a Committee of the House of Commons on London prisons. Her brother-in-law Thomas Fowell Buxton was elected as MP for Weymouth and promoted her work among his fellow MPs. She said that under her system the rules were rarely broken and order was observed – in other words, kindness worked. The women used the money they earnt to buy clothes, and her committee added money to the pot to make sure everyone was covered and decent. Fry also told the committee that the women had only 18in to 2ft of space to lie on at night and said they needed proper dormitories.

In 1818 she travelled throughout the UK and visited prisons, suggesting improvements and setting up committees of female prison visitors. She campaigned for care and rehabilitation after the prison sentences to stop former prisoners reoffending. She also made a huge difference to the way prisoners were taken to the ships that would transport them to Australia; instead of being clapped in irons on open wagons, where they were often stoned or had rotten vegetables thrown at them, she arranged for them to be taken to the ships in closed carriages. She also gave them a 'useful bag' of things they would need. It contained a Bible, a hessian apron, a black apron, a black cotton cap, sewing materials and equipment, a comb, knife and fork, and spectacles. This meant the prisoners could make patchwork quilts on the journey to sell on arrival and also teach the children to read, knit and sew.

Fry also set up a committee to give hot soup and a bed to homeless women and children after a boy was found frozen to death near her home in 1819. Two years later the Ladies' Association became the British Ladies' Society for Promoting the Reformation of Female Prisoners – the first nationwide women's organisation in Britain. Queen Victoria donated £50 towards it and later said that Fry was 'a very superior person'. Together with her brother Joseph John Gurney, Fry tried to get reform on capital punishment. She got nowhere until Robert Peel became the Home Secretary – and then he started to make reforms to the prison service.

But it wasn't all plain sailing for Fry. In 1828 her husband's bank failed. He was disowned by the Quakers because they considered he had put other people's money at risk, even though it wasn't his fault, and the Frys had to move to a smaller house. Joseph Fry was very bitter and refused to wear his Quaker clothes. Elizabeth was deeply hurt by what was happening, but said she couldn't reason on God's will. Years later Joseph Fry was reinstated as a Quaker, but he never quite forgave them for their harshness.

Then, in the 1830s, people started saying that Fry's prison work was 'amateurish'. The Quakers also thought she was neglecting her family and setting too much store by public esteem. She spoke out against solitary confinement to a House of Commons committee in 1832 and was roundly ignored. But this didn't deter her. With her brother's financial support, Fry visited Europe five times between 1838 and 1843 and pleaded for better treatment for prisoners and lunatics, as well as the abolition of slavery in Denmark and the Netherlands. While in Europe she saw a nursing school near Düsseldorf, which influenced her to set up a committee to start a training school for nurses in England when she returned home in 1840. She also set up district visiting societies to work with the poor, and libraries for coastguards.

After several years of poor health, she died on 12 October 1845 in Ramsgate, Kent. Her last words, as her daughter was reading her the Bible, were 'Oh! My dear Lord, help and keep thy servant!' Reportedly 1,000 people attended her funeral and her ideas, although way ahead of her time, gradually filtered in to the prison system.

THIRTEEN

Sarah Glover

Sarah Glover with her Norwich Sol-Fa ladder – drawn in 1879 from a photograph and printed in the Tonic Sol-Fa Jubilee book. *(Photograph by author, courtesy of Norfolk County Council Library and Information Service)*

Most people know the *Do-re-mi* song from *The Sound of Music* – but without Sarah Glover it could never have happened. Sarah Glover was born on 13 November 1786 in The Close, the oldest of four daughters of the Revd Edward Glover. At the age of six she started music lessons with Dr John Beckwith, the organist of Norwich Cathedral. Her father was the curate of St Lawrence's Church in 1811, and she ran a local Sunday school there with her younger sisters Christiana and Margaret.

Glover started to make up a simplified system of musical notation and began pasting guide letters on the piano keys (using alphabetical and sol-fa names) as a development of the Italian solfeggio system. She changed *do, re, mi, fa, sol, la, si* to Doh, Ra, Me, Fah, Sole, Lah and Te (to avoid confusing the identical initials of sol and si). This became known as the Movable Doh system. Glover used it while teaching girls in the school she had set up in Black Boy Yard, Colegate Street, with her sister Christiana. As well as music, the school taught arithmetic, drawing, sewing and music to gentlewomen. Glover also taught in a local charity school.

Harmonicon built for Sarah Glover – held in the collection at Strangers' Hall Museum (viewing by appointment). *(Photograph by kind permission of Norfolk Museums & Archaeology Service (Strangers' Hall Museum)*

Instead of memorising the symbols, the girls sang from the sol-fa notes pointed out on a chart known as Glover's 'Norwich sol-fa ladder.' She had a book of tunes printed in her notations with sol-fa initials and a few additional symbols to represent the accent and duration of notes. Her intention was to 'lead the pupil to sing better in tune, sooner at sight, and to imbibe more correct notations of the theory of music'. A local manufacturer helped her to make a special instrument called a harmonicon, which had 25 glass keys (covering two chromatic octaves) with a roller next to the keys that turned to show the sol-fa symbols for the scale in all 12 keys.

Glover was also interested in including colour in her method. Her assistant Miss Brown said that Glover saw an analogy between colour and sound in the minor scale:

> …that discovered by Sir Isaac Newton to exist between the proportions of the prismatic colours and the divisions of a musical string in the ascending Minor Scale, the space from *Lah* to *Te* being the same as that occupied by violet, the space from *Te* to *Doh* by indigo, from *Doh* to *Ra* by blue, from *Ra* to *Me* by green, from *Me* to *Bah* by yellow, from *Bah* to *Ne* by orange, from *Ne* to the octave above *Lah* by red.

(Bah was the sharp sixth and Ne was the sharp seventh in a minor scale.)

Her ideas were developed from her reading – Hawkins's *A General History of the Science and Practice of Music* published in five volumes in 1776, Newton's *Optics* and J. Marsh's *A Short Introduction to the Theory of Harmonics or the Philosophy of Musical Sounds for the use of such Musical Professors, Amateurs and others, as have not previously studied mathematics.*

There is evidence she began to develop her theory using a 'Philosopher's Whizgig' – a child's toy of the era which had seven segments of colour on one side, seven concentric circles on the other, and string through the middle so it could spin rapidly; the side with coloured segments turned white but the circles on the other side retained their original colour.

Her choir sang in St Lawrence's Church; people asked how it was that the young children could sing so well and asked her to publish her training methods. By 1827 Glover had drawn up a complete method in manuscript form, and in 1835 it was published by Jarrolds as *Scheme for rendering psalmody congregational.*

In 1841 the Congregationalist minister John Spencer Curwen was asked at a conference of Sunday School teachers to find a simple method of teaching singing. He was completely unmusical, so this was a huge challenge for him. He visited Glover's school; he stood outside and heard the children singing – 'such as I had never heard from school children before'. When he went in he saw the child pointing to the notes and singing. He sat up all night with a harmonium and worked through the book of her method; within a fortnight, he had taught himself to sing.

According to Curwen's memoirs of 1882:

> I now saw that Miss Glover's plan was to teach, first, the simple and beautiful *thing*, music, and to delay the introduction to the ordinary antiquated mode of writing it...Her method was, beyond all controversy, more deeply established on the principles of the science than any other...In the course of a fortnight, I found myself, *mirabile dictu!* actually at the height of my previous ambition, being able to 'make out' a psalm-tune from the notes, and to pitch it myself! It was the untying of the tongue – the opening of a new world of pleasure.

Curwen tried the method on children and it worked. They were really enthusiastic so he used the method, adapted it slightly and published it as his own method – but he didn't ask Glover's permission first. A few months later he realised his error and wrote to her, giving her a copy of his book and saying he hoped that she would permit his use of the name 'sol-fa'. Glover's sister Christiana wanted to prosecute him, but Glover replied 'Oh, sister, sister; hold your tongue, and remember we should forgive our enemies, and pray for those who despitefully use us...I am greatly pained at this breach of confidence, but with God's help I will get over the pain.'

Curwen apologised quickly and kept saying he was indebted to Glover, but relations were cool between them. Glover felt that she had taken him in to her school and helped him, and he had betrayed her. He sent her the profits from his first book, but she returned them, saying she had 'never received a pecuniary reward for her work, and did not wish to do so'.

Brass plate commemorating Sarah Glover in St Laurence Church. *(Photograph by author)*
The plaque reads:

To the Glory of God
and to commemorate
the loving labours here and in this city
of Sarah Anna Glover, daughter of the
Revd Edward Glover, formerly rector of this
parish.
She was the author of the Norwich Sol-Fa
System
from which the Tonic Sol-Fa System sprang.
Born Nover 13 1786 Died Octr 20 1867

Beneath this is a line of sol-fa notation, and
then the words:
Sweet is the work, my God, my king, to
praise thy name, give thanks and sing.
Incidentally, they got the details wrong –
Edward Glover was the curate rather than
the rector of St Laurence's.

Glover's niece Mrs Langton Brown, in her memoir of Glover in the Tonic Sol Fa Association's Jubilee publication, said she was small and slight, of much personal charm in her youth, with a fair complexion and bright hair. Glover was near-sighted, so she started to stoop while still young. She was shy and reserved, but also a very good piano player; according to Brown, Glover 'showed as much grasp of harmony as delicacy and fire in rendering the meaning of the composer'. In Brown's view, Glover had a 'tolerant ear' as she liked street-organs and was pleased when people sang psalms, even if their singing was out of tune. She also liked children, 'delighting in their quaint sayings', and Brown added that Glover especially liked naughty children, 'perhaps owing to some dash of originality in their lawlessness'.

Glover walked everywhere and would take her class regardless of the weather, though she wasn't very keen on the country; when she went out for a walk with friends she was visiting in 1853 and realised there were no houses around, she asked if they could go back!

Glover moved to Cromer in 1850, then Reading, then Hereford. She was visiting friends in Great Malvern when she died of a stroke on 20 October 1867 and was buried there. In 1891 the Tonic Sol-Fa association set up a brass plate to Glover's memory in St Lawrence's Church to mark their jubilee.

FOURTEEN

John Grix

John Grix was one of the quiet heroes of Norwich, a shy and retiring character who put other people before himself. Grix was one of five children; his family lived in City Road and he went to St Mark's School in Lakenham. He was a chorister at St Peter Mancroft Church and was also a troop leader in the scouts attached to the church.

His actions in Norwich during the Blitz were incredibly brave, particularly as he had fibbed about his age so that he could become a member of the Civil Defence: he was only 15 at the time. As a member, whenever the air-raid sirens sounded and people took cover, Grix rode off on his bicycle to the report centre to await orders. He took messages to the firemen, even though the incendiary bombs were falling around him. On one occasion he was passing a factory when acid sprayed from the windows and burned his hands; he didn't tell anyone he was hurt and continued taking messages instead. And he didn't stop when the air raid was over; he helped rescuers among the ruins. He slept overnight at the report centre and was out again on the second night of the raid – he kept taking messages, even though he was blown off his bike five times.

Grix simply thought he had been doing his duty and didn't tell anyone at home what he had been doing – but then he received a letter telling him that he was going to receive the British Empire Medal for his bravery. Regional Commissioner Will Spens described Grix as acting 'with courage and determination'. And when King George V visited the city and met Grix, he actually said 'I understand you are only 15'.

Grix received the BEM in September 1942 – and for the rest of his life he never saw himself as a hero, just a man who 'did his bit'.

FIFTEEN

Ralph de Guader

The name of Ralph de Guader is rarely heard in Norwich nowadays – but the Norman castle where he planned to overthrow William the Conqueror still dominates the city's skyline.

After the Norman Conquest it was fairly obvious that William would build a visible symbol of his power in Norwich – firstly because King Harold's brother had been the Earl of East Anglia, and secondly because William Fitz-Osbern (the Earl of Hereford and the joint viceroy in England with Bishop Odo of Bayeux, the Conquerer's half-brother) used Norwich as his eastern headquarters. And what a symbol; according to the *Domesday Book*, nearly 100 houses were destroyed to

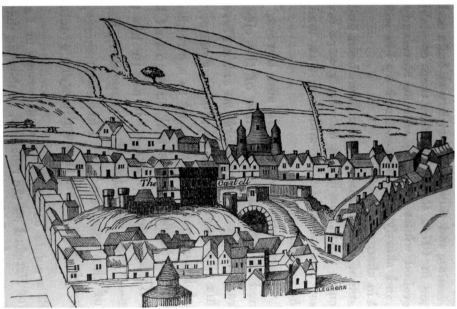

Norwich Castle from Braun's *View of Norwich*, 1581. *(Photograph by author)*

make space for the castle and its earthworks. However, during that period nearly 200 houses in Norwich were standing empty or had fallen into ruin, so it's likely that many of the destroyed houses were in a poor state to start with.

The castle was invested in 1075 and the plan was that a constable would hold the castle in the name of King William. The first constable was Ralph de Guader, who had been born in Norfolk to an English father (who was the staller or horse-master to Edward the Confessor) and a Breton mother. William also made him the Earl of Norfolk and Suffolk. De Guader wasn't particularly popular in England because he was the only English earl to fight on William's side at the Battle of Hastings. When he fell out with Harold, the king made him an outlaw, so in response de Guader led a group of Bretons on the Norman side against him.

De Guader was friendly with William Fitz-Osbern's younger son Roger – a man described by the Anglo-Saxon chroniclers as a 'hateful youth, full of perfidy'. When Fitz-Osbern was killed in Flanders, Roger inherited the earldom of Hereford and the English estates. Shortly after, de Guader decided to marry Emma, the Earl of Hereford's sister.

Hereford had already been in trouble with William. Throughout 1074 Archbishop Lanfranc, the regent, sent Roger several letters rebuking him and reminding him that he should be loyal to his king. Eventually, fed up with the young man's impulsive behaviour and hot-headedness, Lanfranc excommunicated him, saying that he should submit to the king's mercy and make restitution to the king and to any other man he had wronged.

Hereford did nothing of the kind, and in 1075 he permitted Emma to marry de Guader. The king refused flatly to sanction the marriage; it's likely that he realised Hereford and de Guader were dangerous, and he didn't want them joining forces. Worse still, the marriage was celebrated very ostentatiously – which, as they didn't have the king's blessing, was equivalent to flaunting their bad behaviour. The wedding was held at Exning in Cambridgeshire. De Guader's Breton friends attended, along with bishops and abbots – who really should have had nothing to do with the excommunicate Earl of Hereford, let alone agreed to be his guest at the 'bride-ale'.

As the *Anglo-Saxon Chronicle* put it:

Þær wes Þæt bryd eala   mannum to beala
(There was that bride ale, which was many man's bale.)

Huge amounts of beer and wine were drunk. The guests started to complain about William and, according to the *Anglo-Saxon Chronicle*, took advice about 'how they might drive their lord out of the kingdom'.

Hereford was already set against William; de Guader, as his new brother-in-law, was bound to help him. Waltheof, the Earl of Northumberland, Northampton and Huntingdon, was also at the party. He had joined a Danish attack on York only three years after submitting to William after the Battle of Hastings, so Hereford and de Guader saw him as a natural part of their plot – even though Waltheof had married William's niece, Judith, and so should have been firmly on William's side.

Hereford and de Guader's proposal was that they should drive William out of the country, then divide the country into three. One of them would rule as the king, while the other two would remain earls; each would have a third of the country.

The next morning, once Waltheof had sobered up (and possibly talked to his wife), he thought better of it and confessed to Lanfranc. Lanfranc made him do penances for the church, then told Waltheof he had to go to Normandy and explain the situation to William. Waltheof went to France, laden with gifts, and asked William to forgive him. William appeared to do so and kept Waltheof with him, under extremely close supervision.

Meanwhile, de Guader and Hereford rebelled openly. De Guader asked his family in Brittany and Denmark to help him. English Bretons came to his aid, and King Sweyn sent de Guader a fleet under the command of his son Cnut and Earl Hakon.

Lanfranc moved swiftly to crush the rebellion and called the rest of England to his aid. According to the chronicler Simeon of Jarrow, Wulfstan, the bishop of Worcester, joined forces with Aethelwig, the abbot of Evesham, and together they prevented Hereford crossing over the Severn to join de Guader's forces. Odo, the bishop of Bayeux, and Geoffrey, bishop of Coutance, went into battle against de Guader just outside Cambridge. Realising that his forces weren't strong enough to resist them, de Guader fled back to Norwich – and Lanfranc reported to William that *Rodolfus traditur* (Ralph the traitor) and his army were fleeing, and the king's men were chasing him.

Hereford was captured and imprisoned. Waltheof was also put in prison; although he hadn't actually done anything rebellious and had told William everything he knew, William saw Waltheof as a danger to the country because he had listened to traitors – particularly when Waltheof's old Danish comrades were in the vicinity. Not that the Danes did much – according to the *Anglo-Saxon*

Chronicle, the fleet of 200 ships decided that it wasn't strong enough to fight William, so Cnut went to York and looted St Peter's Minster instead.

De Guader entrusted the castle and a garrison to Emma's hands and fled to Brittany by ship – at the time there was an estuary from Yarmouth meadows to Harford Bridges, so shipping links to Norwich were very good. From Brittany de Guader travelled to Denmark, hoping for aid from the Danish side of his family. Meanwhile, bishops Odo of Bayeux and Geoffrey de Coutance laid siege to Norwich Castle.

Emma would have had good cause to throw her lot in with William. Her grandfather had been William's guardian; her father had been William's best friend; and her family were connected to the dukes of Normandy. But she must have loved de Guader very much, because instead she defended the castle with her garrison of Armorican Bretons, even though there was no sign of help from her husband or the promised Danish and Breton ships.

According to the 19th-century historian A.D. Bayne, the castle 'was much injured' during the siege. But Emma and her garrison held out for three months until starvation finally forced them to surrender. Lanfranc was so impressed by her bravery that he negotiated a very fair settlement with her; he gave her 40 days to leave the country forever. At the Severn, Odo of Bayeux, Geoffrey de Coutance, Richard de Bienfait and William de Warenne cut off the right foot of every prisoner they made – meaning that they wouldn't be able to ride again – but, thanks to Emma, the people at Norwich were admitted to terms rather than mutilated or cast out.

William followed Ralph to Brittany and besieged him in his castle at Dol. However, Alan Feargent, the Duke of Bretagne, and King Philip of France came to Ralph's aid and William had to give up. The *Anglo-Saxon Chronicle* notes that William lost 'men and horses and much treasure'. William also ended up negotiating a treaty that meant the Duke of Bretagne would marry William's daughter Constance.

Lanfranc wrote to William saying that the realm was cleared from the 'infection' of 'Breton scum', adding that:

> The landless mercenaries who served Ralph the traitor and his associates begged for and were granted the same terms within the limit of one month. Bishop Geoffrey, William of Warenne and Robert Malet have remained in the castle itself with 300 heavily armed soldiers, supported by a large force of slingers and siege engineers.

Ralph's rebellion was over. Emma, taking advantage of the terms she had negotiated with Lanfranc, joined de Guader in Brittany and they lived quietly for the next 20 years. She joined him when he went on the First Crusade in 1096. De Guader died at some point between Nicaea and Jerusalem, and it's assumed that Emma died with him.

At the Midwinter Gemot or parliament on 25 December 1075, Hereford and Waltheof were brought to trial. De Guader was condemned in his absence. Hereford was imprisoned for life, fined heavily and his lands confiscated. His followers were punished by having their eyes put out or their hands cut off; some were banished, some were 'put to shame' and others hung in a gibbet.

Waltheof defended himself; his sentence was deferred and he was kept in prison in Winchester until the Pentecostal Gemot or parliament of 1076. Again he argued his case, but he was beheaded on 31 May and subsequently became a martyr, with signs and wonders seen at his tomb in Crowland.

As for Norwich's punishment, the *Domesday Book* says that 32 burgesses fled the town and others were ruined by confiscation of their property. The yearly 'farm' (the lease of the revenues from tolls and court fines) that the burgesses had to pay to the king was tripled to £90. After Christmas at Westminster, William decided to punish all who had attended de Guader's wedding in Norwich – some had their eyes put out, some were banished and some had to forfeit all they had.

Ralph de Guader is forgotten; however, his coat of arms forms the lower part of Norfolk County Council's arms today.

SIXTEEN

George Harmer

George Harmer was one of the coldest-blooded killers Norwich has ever known. His apprehension involved a joint operation of the Metropolitan Police and Scotland Yard.

The victim was 66-year-old Henry Last, a retired master carpenter who lived in School Lane. He was thin, badly dressed and kept pigeons in one room – but was actually very well off because he rented out the adjoining properties.

Around 10.30 to 11.30 on the morning of Saturday 14 August 1886, neighbour Catherine Richmond saw a man knocking on Last's door. There was no answer, so the man asked her if Last was home. When she said she didn't know, he walked off and said he would call again. She noticed that he was carrying a piece of board to Last's house. He returned and entered the house, then left 30 minutes later. She didn't see him leave but heard the door bang and footsteps going out of the yard.

Another neighbour, Rachel Curl, went to pay her rent to Last at around 1pm; she knew he would be at home as that was when he usually fed his chickens. She noticed the door was ajar; she kept ringing the bell, and when there was no answer she called in through the door. Again there was no answer, and the chickens were waiting outside. She fed them at 2pm but didn't look for Last, assuming he'd gone out somewhere. Neighbour Mrs Challis also called later in the afternoon, but left again when Last didn't reply.

At 8pm neighbour Henry Chilvers was concerned when he saw that Last's door was still open. He went to find Last's friend Peter Hoydahl, who went into the house, found a light and saw a pile of sacks. Lying underneath them was Henry Last's body. They went to the police station just up the road at the Guildhall. The police returned with a lantern, lifted the body and put it on a trestle. They saw wounds on the back of Last's head and over his right eye, and a pool of blood on the floor. DI Robert Mason noticed a board with the centre cut out, but nobody could think why it was there. Hoydahl showed him Last's hidden safe, which was locked – and they couldn't find the key.

Dr Robert Mills, the police surgeon, did the post mortem. He said there had been six or seven blows to the back of Last's head and three to the front near his eyes. Some of the blows had penetrated his brain and cracked his skull into nine pieces. Mills thought the murder weapon was some kind of hammer.

At Thorpe railway station, prison warder Benjamin Munford saw George Harmer, a 26-year-old plasterer who had been released from prison that morning. Harmer said that his father had given him money, and he was going to Yarmouth; then he changed his story and claimed he was going to the Isle of Wight.

Harmer had been released at 7am after doing a month's hard labour for assaulting his wife. He went back home to Scoles Green, where his neighbour Sarah Kemp invited him in for breakfast. When Harmer asked where his wife was, Sarah gave him a note from her saying that she'd left him. He started crying, at which point, Sarah gave him a clean handkerchief and 3d to get a shave, and then he went to neighbour Mary Savage and spent an hour talking about his wife.

Around half-past nine Harmer went to the house of his friend Edward Nelson in Lower Westwick Street. Nelson was a saw maker by trade but had been convicted for poaching. Harmer had breakfast there and said he wouldn't do any more work until he had found his wife, but meanwhile he would get some money by 'rob[bing] old Last'. Harmer asked Nelson for a pencil and a piece of wood on which to draw a pattern, but Nelson refused to give him any wood. Harmer tried to steal a board from a cart Nelson was working on and even Mrs Nelson's scrubbing board! Finally they sent him packing; he went to James Mace's cabinetmaking shop at Charing Cross and asked for some nails and a piece of wood, claiming it was for Nelson. Then he returned to Nelson's house to mark out a pattern on the board with a file. When Nelson asked why, Harmer said it was 'to attract the old man's attention'. He showed Nelson a plasterer's hammer and said 'I shall hit the old —— on the head and daze him.'

He spent the next hour or so drinking rum in the New Corn Exchange pub in Bedford Street. Then, just before 1pm, Harmer returned to Nelson's place, sweating and shaky and looking very excited. He no longer had the board with him. When Nelson asked what he had done, Harmer said, 'I've just been and done the job, robbing old Last.' Nelson ordered him off his premises; Harmer wrapped guns, a knife and rings in a handkerchief and left. Later that afternoon labourer

John Smith pawned Harmer's revolver and pistol in the name of John Carter, while Harmer waited outside. They returned to Harmer's house and fetched a telescope, a blanket and a counterpane to pawn at another shop; the telescope was refused but Harmer got money for the rest. He then sold a powder flask to a broker in Timberhill and bought back the suit he had pawned the previous year.

Next, Harmer went to see Mrs Kemp and Mrs Savage and told them he was selling up. He asked if they wanted to buy anything, but they refused; so he went to furniture broker William Scott in Timberhill, who came back to the house with him and bought the furniture. Harmer asked Mrs Savage to look after a box for him and send it when he wrote to her, because he was going to London to find his wife. He left on the 2pm Sunday train.

Meanwhile, the police were investigating Last's murder and bringing in suspects. On Tuesday 17 August Nelson went to the police and told them what he knew. He said he hadn't come to them the previous day because he didn't think Harmer had murdered Last, but then he saw that 'innocent people were being taken' so he thought he'd better tell them.

Mrs Savage received a letter asking for Harmer's box to be sent to 'George Smith' at Wandsworth railway station. Her husband bound the box and labelled it, and together they took it to the railway station. When they came home, the police were waiting for them. Detective Inspector Mason went straight to the railway station and found the box; Chief Constable Robert Hitchman told him to follow the box and meanwhile telegraphed the Metropolitan Police. Mason followed the box and waited at the station until midnight. When the box wasn't claimed, he went to Scotland Yard.

Harmer had talked his landlady, Rachel Dale, into collecting his box on the Thursday morning. As soon as she asked for it, plain clothes policemen at the station collared her and asked questions. Meanwhile, other police were waiting outside for Harmer. They saw Mrs Dale gesture to him – and, 50 yards away from the police cordon, Harmer ran. Unfortunately for him, he ran straight towards Constable Bennett, who reached out with his umbrella and collared the suspect. He was promptly arrested, and Mason told him he was being taken to Norwich on suspicion of murdering Henry Last. Harmer claimed he knew nothing about it; however, they opened his box to find tools (including a plasterer's hammer) and clothes. Harmer's wife saw him at the police station, and he said he was running away because he owed money to people, not that he had done anything wrong.

News spread and crowds were waiting at Norwich station expecting to see the criminal brought back from London to justice. But the police managed to avoid the hordes by stopping the train at Trowse rather than Thorpe and taking Harmer back to the city in a cab.

Despite the evidence, Harmer claimed that he had been at Ashby all Saturday and had nothing to do with the murder. The inquest had to be adjourned when one of the jury fainted as details of Last's injuries were made clear. And then John Smith came forward with the keys which Harmer had given him; two of them fitted Last's safe. During the examination, although the question wasn't asked, it was made obvious to everyone that Smith had been in prison for the previous six months and had come out on the Wednesday before the murder.

Within 10 minutes of retiring, the jury had reached a verdict of guilty. The judge called it 'one of the worst events which had happened in the criminal history of the city for many years'. Harmer called out that he was innocent, but nobody believed him. The *Norfolk Chronicle*'s verdict was that 'there is not a single mitigating circumstance in the whole case' and 'a murder was never perpetrated in colder blood'.

Finally, the weekend before he was due to be executed, Harmer admitted his guilt. He confessed to several crimes as well as the murder and told the prison governor that he had intended 'to smash the old man' and 'have no nonsense about it'.

Harmer was executed on 13 December 1886 at Norwich Castle, and he was the last person to be executed there.

SEVENTEEN

Father Ignatius

Father Ignatius. *(Picture courtesy of Norfolk County Council Library and Information Service)*

Father Ignatius is one of the strangest characters Norwich has ever known. It is difficult to say whether he's a villain, a victim or a hero – or even all three. The two years he spent in the city gave rise to a lot of anger (and a lot of lampooning), and he did irreparable damage to one of the city's churches. He was careless with money, fell desperately ill every time he was challenged (perhaps a form of manic depression, so maybe it wasn't all manipulation), and yet he had close friends who were adamant that he was kind and gentle, and all he really wanted to do was to become a monk.

He was born on 23 November 1837 in London, with the given name of Joseph Leycester Lyne. He went to prep school in Holloway where, at the age of eight, he saw the ghost of a schoolmate who had died in the room next to his. At the age of 10 he went to St Paul's School, where he had a nervous breakdown after being given 42 strokes of the cane by the Surmaster, Revd J.P. Bean. Incredibly, the reason was that Lyne had been looking at pictures of the Temple in Jersualem instead of his textbook. The doctor ordered a year's rest; his parents took him away in 1852 to finish his education at private schools in Spalding and Worcester, and the young Lyne became very interested in the theatre and music as well as religion.

He studied theology at Trinity College, Glenalmond, and he began to think about establishing an order of Anglican monks; but he was worried about his academic prowess (and his teachers were more impressed with his piety than his ability to learn) and in 1856 had another breakdown because of his fear of failing. He was also terrified of going to hell and claimed later in his autobiography that he became a monk to save his soul.

Lyne became a catechist in Inverness, but clashed with Bishop Eden and his parishioners. In 1860 he was ordained as a deacon in Exeter, on the condition that he remained a deacon for three years and didn't preach in the diocese of Exeter. He became an unpaid curate at St Peter's in Plymouth. He also founded the Society of the Love of Jesus, based on monastic principles, and called himself Brother Joseph.

He fell ill again and travelled to Belgium to visit monasteries there. He also started wearing a Benedictine habit. When he returned to London, he was in charge of a mission church, but came under pressure to stop wearing monastic robes; his response was to resign. (During this period in Whitechapel he also claimed to raise Lizzie Meek, who had died of typhoid, from the dead – though nothing was reported in the press.) In 1862 he tried to establish a monastic community at Claydon, near Ipswich, but he was threatened by protestors and the bishop of Norwich refused him a licence to preach.

Norwich attracted his attention. At first he considered using Samson and Hercules House on Tombland, but then he discovered premises on Elm Hill which had previously been occupied by the Dominicans and were at the time leased as a warehouse. He managed to lease it (in the name of lime-burner Stephen Balls) for a £50 deposit, moved in on 30 January 1864, and established the Priory of St Mary and St Dunstan. The sole inhabitants of the monastery were Lyne – by this time known as Father Ignatius – and Brother Dunstan, plus Lyne's dog. Having no money, they lived on bread and potatoes, and they couldn't afford to put glass into the broken windows or locks on the doors. But kind-hearted locals rallied round and helped to fix the building, brought them food and fuel, and even a doctor offered his services free.

The first night Ignatius said the Nocturns, the bell began to toll by itself (though this was probably the wind or rats). Then there were other supernatural events: a fire in the chapel with a voice telling Ignatius to put it out; a blue flame that vanished when the sign of the cross was made; the figure on the crucifix moved; and a mob tried to burn the house down but a thunderstorm doused the

The Monastery in Elm Hill.
(Photograph by author)

flames. However, much of this could be attributed to coincidence or even mass hysteria, because passions ran high.

Ignatius converted Edwin Hillyard, the rector of nearby St Lawrence's Church, to his views. Hillyard let him take part in the services and allowed the monks to go there for daily Communion, which was practically unknown at the time, even in Catholic churches. To everyone's shock – because they weren't used in the Church of England at the time – the services included candles, vestments and incense. It didn't stop there; Ignatius was unhappy that the parishioners had to pay a rent for a pew in St Lawrence's, because he felt it stopped poor people worshipping, and he told Hillyard to abolish the pews. When Hillyard didn't immediately obey, Ignatius and his followers chopped up the box pews, removed the reredos and put in screens and altar steps. The churchwarden complained to the bishop about Ignatius and his attitude to church furniture; the next morning, he was found dead.

Many people believed in him; many didn't. And a kind of hysteria swept the city. There were broadsheets posted everywhere, with titles such as 'strange doings on Elm Hill, or Monkery in Norwich'. One particular broadsheet, entitled *Elm Hill Menagerie*, talks of the great attractions there: 'a number of Monk He's & Monk She's' and 'the man with two faces' (i.e. Ignatius – one thing to some people and one to others). The broadsheet also mentions the 'Holy Water to be collected and preserved in a tub, by Ignatius, is having peculiar effects on softening the brain.'

There was a huge row in September 1864 when one of the choirboys – a printer's apprentice called Hase – wanted to join them and threw up his apprenticeship. His step-mother disapproved of the monastery in any case, but also clearly thought homosexual practices were involved. She forbade the boy to attend services, but the boy soon came back, claiming she had changed her mind, and Ignatius didn't check with his mother until the boy said he wanted to become a postulant. At this point Ignatius wrote to Mrs Hase, who refused to give her approval, and he took it as Protestant bias. He let the boy stay, and Mrs Hase consequently went to the papers. The *Norfolk News* printed a letter that one of

St Laurence's Church. *(Photograph by author)*

the monks, Augustine, had sent to the boy, addressed to 'My Darling Child' and containing lines such as 'you will *never* realise how much I really love you, and how wretched I am all day without seeing you' and asking the boy to have his portrait taken for him. Ignatius claimed the letter was written 'during a temporary fit of insanity' and expelled Augustine – not for writing the love letter but for doing it secretly and attempting to procure a photograph without permission, which Ignatius said broke two of the house rules.

The problem blew over, but Ignatius still had financial troubles. At the end of 1864 he managed to get a loan to buy the Elm Hill property, but he claimed he was 'an ass about business' (in a letter to the *Evening Standard* appealing for funds), and the property was to be conveyed to Mr Drury, his patron.

At this point Ignatius was becoming ill again, and his mother came to Norwich to look after him. She wasn't impressed by his Infant Oblate (the child of a woman whose husband had left her with three children and no money – Ignatius called him 'Baby Ignatius' and dressed the little boy in a white habit and cowl), saying, 'He has a very curious disposition, and not a nice one.' She wasn't impressed by the other brothers at the monastery either.

There was another row when a ball was held at St Andrew's Hall. Ignatius believed it was blasphemy to hold a ball in the church of the Black Friars (even though it hadn't been that since the Dissolution) and forbade his followers to attend. Hillyard and some others went, but one of the brothers from the Priory was sent to tell them to leave. They refused, and their names were taken. During the Sunday service, Ignatius named all of the offenders and told them they had to make public penance. The women had to lie in ashes on the floor, the older men had to hold a 'tallow dip' candle in their right hands before the congregation and the younger men were to be caned publicly by Ignatius on the altar steps. Mr Utton Browne wrote to Ignatius asking him to let his wife, son and daughter off the punishment, but Ignatius refused and the three did their penance. Browne stopped supporting Ignatius after that. Ignatius excommunicated Hillyard from the priory, which meant he and his monks couldn't go back to St Lawrence's. So instead they went to St Saviour's; the Revd Cooke protested to the bishop and was told he didn't have to give communion to anyone wearing 'their ridiculous dress'.

The Anglican church still refused to ordain Ignatius as a priest because of his monastic habit; they felt that it was likely to cause problems with parishioners, just as it had in Ipswich. In June 1865 Ignatius tried to get Samuel Wilberforce, the bishop of Oxford, on his side and force the bishop of Norwich to give communion to the monks; however, he was disappointed as Wilberforce told him to obey the bishop of Norwich, and added that former monks 'took the dress to help the work' but Ignatius 'mar[red] the work to have the dress'. Wilberforce tried to persuade Ignatius away from the path of self-destruction; instead of listening, Ignatius wrote back and refuted every single point the bishop had made.

Ignatius then went on a fund-raising mission in London, putting a novice in charge, but just before that he imposed a harsh penance on his community for breaking his rule of 'Solemn Silence' – he made them trace a cross on the ground with their tongues.

While he was in London, Brother Marcus – who had been with the priory for just one day – rebelled and deposed Ignatius as the superior. His reasons were because of the penance, the fact he didn't like being so subservient, and the fact that all letters written and received at the monastery were supervised. But the congregation stoned Marcus when he tried to preach. Ignatius returned, gave him and Brother Stanislaus (another of the rebels) £5 each and told them to leave. The rest of the brotherhood were put under a penance and pardoned, and then Ignatius went off on another mission.

Next, he attended the Church Congress at Bristol and put his case for monasticism to them, but he made it clear he wouldn't consider any other type of religious order except his own. And then he held a public meeting in Bristol, which convinced various bishops that he was going to do more harm than good to the church.

Having got nowhere in arguing his cause, he returned to Norwich and started making miracles. He cured an epileptic woman with water in which he had dipped a medal of St Benedict, and he eased another of toothache with a scrap of wool from his scapular. A woman who cursed him in the street fell dead in a doorway. Another teased him about his tonsure, and her child's hair fell out immediately; then Ignatius restored it when she begged him to help.

But two months after the 'mutiny' his financial problems reared their head again. His response was a cataleptic fit and 'visions' of a square 4ft high demon with a head like a turnip. He was ill in bed for a fortnight, and then he went to convalesce at Margate. He returned to Norwich two months later but had clearly had enough; he broke down again near the end of December and claimed he could hear angels singing and was about to die. He recovered and decided to go to Jerusalem but, on the way, he collapsed in Paris. Another recovery got him to Rome, where he had an audience with Pope Pius IX – who told him 'the cowl doesn't make the monk'. Ignatius had a ready retort: that the *life* made the monk (except Ignatius didn't actually live it).

He continued abroad until May 1866, worrying when he realised that the £500 to buy the priory on Elm Hill had been a loan rather than a gift – and he had no money. He wrote to Mr Drury in Norwich from Brussels and discovered that the priory was over £1,000 in debt. A few days later he wrote back to Drury and asked him to tell everyone that his health was poor and he couldn't 'return to Norwich or have anything more to do with the Mission there', at least until the business side of things had been sorted out. He claimed that since he had been ill nobody had tried to raise funds, and he was hopeful that someone would offer a retreat to him and the brothers at Norwich. Drury pointed out that they had been raising money, but Ignatius had squandered an awful lot of it; and if he wanted the monastery to continue, he would have to return and raise the money for the new buildings he had bought.

Predictably, Ignatius collapsed and had to return to his parents' home. Meanwhile, Mr Drury took over the priory, helped the three resident monks with food and clothing and started repair work on the buildings, which had become structurally dangerous because of the conversion work. Ignatius was happy to let his father claim he had been swindled out of the property (which he had never actually paid for), but when the case went to court it was shown that he had signed only a tenancy agreement and had no claim to the property. Drury said that repair work and settling outstanding bills cost £1,300; he had taken out a mortgage for the amount, and his mortgagers were happy to sell it to Ignatius for £1,200. Ignatius refused (even though he had a reversionary claim on a rich relative's estate) and wanted it taken to arbitration. Drury had nothing to hide and agreed. When it seemed that the arbitrators were going to pass judgement in Drury's favour, Ignatius's solicitor advised him to abide by the decision and not to go to court or he would lose and it would cost a fortune.

But Ignatius did it his way. He appealed to the Lord Chancellor, and the arbitrators said that there had been no collusion, and Drury had acted 'with perfect honour and good faith'. Ignatius went back to Norwich and took occupation of the priory. Drury didn't attempt to evict him, and Ignatius continued with his bill in chancery. Drury answered every point – and then Louisa Stone, who had lent the original £500, wrote to him saying the charges were unfounded, and she would never have lent the money if she had realised Ignatius intended to buy it for his benefit and not to establish an order of monks. Finally Ignatius agreed he couldn't take it to open court, and the case was dismissed. He eventually established a monastery at Llanthony in the Black Mountains, South Wales. Friends donated money to help him build the monastery, and he preached up and down the country, earning more money to spend on the buildings. However, he didn't attract that many members and was in court in 1873 for allowing a young ward of the Chancery court to become a novice at the abbey.

In March 1876 when the priory on Elm Hill was up for sale, Ignatius was furious. He complained it couldn't possibly be for sale as it was his property, and he didn't want a religious house turned into an upholsterer's workshop because that would be sacrilegious. On receiving a lawyer's letter in June outlining his legal position (i.e. that he had no case), Ignatius went back to the priory and broke into the chapel. He revested the altar, and the monks were singing in the choir when the sheriff's officers banged on the locked door and demanded that he opened it. Ignatius said they were in a service and wanted the officers to wait until he had finished. The second the service was over, the eviction notice was served – but Ignatius said he wouldn't budge unless he was removed by force. The officers duly took him outside; in front of the magistrate, he was bound over to keep the peace for 30 days. He still complained that the priory was stolen from him, but he agreed not to enter the premises for 30 days. Meanwhile, he wrote to the solicitor threatening that if he allowed the property taken from him by fraud to be turned into an upholsterer's workshop then he would be cursed. He delivered sermons in the Rampant Horse pub, and returned to Llanthony.

His death was reported in error in February 1890. He finally passed away at his sister's house in Camberley in 1908, aged 71. *The Times*, in their obituary, summed him up as a man who 'had great gifts of utterance, great powers of riveting the attention of men as well as women. What he lacked was that sense of system and of discipline which comes out of careful education'.

And the curse?

Allegedly, people have seen Ignatius walking up and down Elm Hill, carrying a large black Bible and cursing anyone who passes by...

EIGHTEEN

Julian of Norwich

Statue of Mother Julian at Norwich Cathedral. *(Photograph by author)*

Julian of Norwich is well known as a mystic and the writer of the first book in English by a woman, *Revelations of Divine Love*. She was born around 1342; not much is known about her life, though it is unlikely that she was a nun in nearby Carrow Priory as nobody in the priory fits her name or circumstances at the time.

Julian prayed to God to give her three gifts, if it was his will. Firstly, she wanted to witness Christ's Passion, so she could suffer with Jesus and truly understand his Passion; secondly, she wanted to be ill when she was 30 (the same age as Christ was when he started his ministry) and to be near death, so she would be given the last rites and be cleansed and could therefore lead a more consecrated life afterwards; and thirdly, she wanted three 'internal wounds', by which she meant true contrition, natural compassion and an unshakeable longing for God.

On 8 May 1373, Julian was aged 30 and it was the fourth day of a serious illness; everyone believed she was dying, and she was given the last rites. Her mother leaned over to close her eyes – Julian was looking at a crucifix at the time – and Julian thought she was about to die when suddenly she felt well again. She began having a series of 16 visions of Christ's suffering (the Passion) and the Blessed Virgin. When she was better, she wrote down an account of her visions. She also wrote a second version, the *Book of Shewings*, years later when she was able to understand her visions – as she put it, 'twenty yere save thre monthys' – and during that time she also had extra visions, firstly in 1388 and then again in 1393.

In her first vision Julian saw red blood trickling down from the thorns pressed into Christ's head. Then she saw a hazelnut in the palm of her hand and asked God what it was. He told her that it was 'all that is made'; she believed that it represented everything she could see and touch and that God made it, loves it and keeps it. Next, she had a vision of Christ on the cross; her language is very unusual here because she talks about the dried-out body. She also takes the unusual viewpoint of discussing Christ as 'mother' – and calls herself 'a simple creature unlettered'. Then she had a vision that sin stood in her way of God; therefore, without sin, she would have been pure and like God. However, all the way through the vision she is reassured that all would be well, and the final assertion of the book is incredibly uplifting: 'all shall be well, and all shall be well, and all manner of things shall be well'.

The visions made Julian decide to become an anchoress rather than a nun, and to devote her life totally to God. The anchorite's cell at St Julian's Church

Cell of Mother Julian at St Julian's Church. *(Photograph by author)*

off King Street was vacant, so she moved there, and it's also possible that she took her name from the church. She lived there according to the 'Ancren Riwle' of recluses, which meant that she could have a servant and two meals a day (though they couldn't include flesh or lard) and could keep a cat. The rule also said that her cell should have three windows: one into the church, so she could hear Mass and receive the sacrament; one to communicate with her servant; and one to give advice to people who asked her for it. One of the people who visited her was another famous Norfolk woman:

Margery Kempe, the mystic of Lynn, who came to Norwich in 1413. Kempe visited Julian because 'the anchoress was expert in such things and could give good counsel'.

Julian's God was merciful and believed in love rather than vengeance. In her revelation of 1388 she states:

> You would know our Lord's meaning in this thing? Know it well. Love was his meaning. Who showed it to you? Love. What did he show you? Love. Why did he show it? For love. Hold on to this and you will know and understand love more and more.

Close-up of stained glass at Mother Julian's cell. *(Photograph by author)*

Julian died in about 1416. Her cell was pulled down during the Reformation; St Julian's Church was bombed during the Baedeker Raids of 1942 and was razed to the ground, except for the high altar, reredos and tabernacle. The church was rebuilt incorporating the Norman archway from the nearby church of St Michael at Thorn, which was also destroyed in the raids. When the area was excavated, foundations were discovered which were thought to belong to the original cell, so the cell was rebuilt at the same time as the church.

She was never formally beatified as a saint, but 8 May is the day when she is commemorated in the Church of England calendar.

NINETEEN

Robert Kett

1549 was the summer of discontent. Taxation was rising to pay for the war with France and Scotland; unemployment was rising as landowners switched from arable farming to sheep farming to meet the demand for wool, and therefore only needed one shepherd instead of 10 labourers; rents were rising and the local gentry were

Kett's Oak, on the old A11 between Wymondham and Hethersett. *(Photograph by author)*

fencing off the common lands, a practice known as enclosure. (Although the common lands actually belonged to the lord of the manor, he was meant to leave enough land unenclosed so that his freehold tenants could graze their stock; however, as most tenants weren't freehold, their needs were ignored.) Add droughts, food shortages and a huge rise in the population, and it was hardly surprising that the poorer people had had enough and rebelled. During the summer people all over the country were destroying hedges and fences put up by landlords.

Kett was an unlikely rebel: elderly, married with five children, a major landowner (he had three manors in Wymondham) and law-abiding, he had much to do with the church. He was 57 when the rebellion started, and at the time the average life expectancy was 32. (Even if you take out the skewing for the high infant mortality – around 25 per cent of children died before their fifth birthday, and a further 25 per cent of people died before the age of 25 – the average person only lived to around the age of 65, a mere eight years older than Kett.)

He didn't see himself as a rebel, however. It may have been his involvement in guilds and their principles of social justice and order that prompted him to join the rebels, but it may also have had something to do with his longstanding arguments with Hethersett lawyer John Flowerdew. Flowerdew stole the lead from the roof and some of the stone of Wymondham Abbey after Henry VIII closed the abbey; this damaged the parish church, as its nave was left open to the elements, and it also ignored the agreement between the king and the town. Kett was furious about this because he was

Cow tower, part of the city defences damaged during Kett's rebellion. *(Photograph by author)*

heavily involved with the local church and had formerly been in charge of the altar vessels and candles. He was also part of the group of townspeople who collected money to buy back the bells and lead, and Flowerdew had made it very difficult for them. In addition, Flowerdew owed money to Kett's elder brother William.

The rebellion started at the Wymondham Fair on 6 July 1549. The townsfolk had been entertained with mystery plays and processions and had had much to eat and drink. At this point, people started to grumble about taxation and local government, and a group of people went off to Morley on 8 July to pull down fences belonging to John Hobart before doing the same with Flowerdew's fences in Hethersett. Flowerdew pointed out that Kett had started to enclose common land near the Fairland in Wymondham, and offered the mob 40 pence to pull Kett's fences down. But instead of stopping the people from destroying the fences, Kett clearly realised how unfair the practice of enclosure was. He said 'Whatever lands I have enclosed shall be made common unto ye and all men, and my own hand shall first perform it.' He joined the mob in pulling down the fences, and then made sure they ripped down Flowerdew's. He even said that he was ready 'to sacrifice my substance' and 'my very life itself' in the cause – so he was clearly a man who believed in doing what was right, even though it would be at personal cost to himself.

On 9 July 1549 a crowd assembled under an oak tree between Wymondham and Hethersett, and Kett led the march to the city. He established a camp on

Mousehold Heath on 12 July and was joined by 15,000 men from Norfolk. Although one of the hostile chroniclers of the rebellion claimed that Kett's rebels ate 20,000 sheep, 4,000 oxen and thousands of poultry in just a few days, it's highly unlikely they consumed anywhere near that amount; besides, Kett banned all looting. He held a court of justice on the heath under a tree known as the Oak of Reformation. Trials were open and fair, and nobody was killed or injured. There were also daily religious services.

Kett and his followers drew up a list of 29 requests which, to modern eyes, were completely fair and just. Enclosure wasn't their only grievance. The rebels asked the king to stop the practice of enclosures and rack renting, to make the measurements of bushels the same throughout the country (eight gallons), to remove priests who didn't preach properly and to make those earning more than £10 a year teach the children of the poor. Their most famous request was that 'all bond men may be made free, for God made all free with his precious blood shedding' – although Kett was a landowner he didn't forget the villeins. The rebels didn't want to overthrow society, they simply wanted to make it socially and economically just. Holinshed's view of the rebels were that they were 'wicked caitiffs' and ignorant, but the list shows they were far from it. Kett was rebelling against injustices of local government and naively thought that London would support him.

A royal herald offered Kett and his followers a pardon on 21 July, provided they disbanded. Kett refused, saying 'Kings and princes are wont to pardon wicked persons, not innocent and just men. We...are guilty ourselves of no crime.' The city gates were closed against the rebels, and Kett offered a truce; it was rejected, so he attacked the city and captured it on 22 July. Any looting was quickly stopped, and there was little destruction of property. Any captured men were simply held prisoner, not killed or harmed.

On 31 July the Earl of Northampton brought his army. The royal herald ordered Kett to surrender, but he refused. A three-hour battle ensued. According to a near-contemporary account by Alexander Neville, 'Many [rebels] were drowned in their own and other men's blood.' Three hundred rebels died, and the rebels withdrew to Mousehold.

On 1 August Northampton offered them another pardon at Pockthorpe Gate, but again it was refused as the rebels said they weren't traitors – they simply wanted economic justice. Meanwhile, another section of the rebels captured the royal cannon on Bishopsgate Bridge, and Northampton's deputy Lord Sheffield was killed. Then the rebels occupied and garrisoned Norwich.

The chronicler Sotherton says that the rebels looted shops and warehouses; however, a wealthy city such as Norwich would surely have been wrecked and pillaged after being in the hands of 20,000 rebels for three weeks. The fact that it wasn't ruined shows that Kett kept order. He also reinstated Augustine Steward, the deputy mayor, as the civic leader. He knew that another royal army would arrive and tried twice to capture Yarmouth – firstly on 5 August and then again on 17 August – to increase his power base, but failed.

On 18 August the Earl of Warwick marched with a 7,500-strong army, joined by the gentry of Essex, Suffolk and Norfolk. The army was 12,000 strong when he arrived at Norwich on 24 August. The herald offered a pardon to all bar Kett, but then called them a 'vile and horrible company' and said if they didn't accept the pardon they would be crushed. The rebels were angered because they thought the pardon wouldn't be honoured. Kett tried to quieten the situation by asking the herald to read the pardon again, but then, as chronicler Ralph Holinshed put it, 'There was a vile boy that turned up his bare tail to him, with words as unseemly as his gesture was filthy.' The herald's irritated bodyguard shot the boy. The rebels were in uproar and refused to let Kett go with the herald. He was torn between standing by his men and trying to negotiate a settlement and avoid more bloodshed, and the herald wasn't much help, simply telling him, 'Stay this concourse and tumult.'

Warwick forced his way into the city and hanged 49 rebels in the market place (the chamberlain's accounts refer to 8 pence to make a 'pair of gallows' and 3 shillings and 9 pence for burying the men in pits) and although the rebels captured most of his artillery in Bishopgate when his soldiers got lost near Tombland, 300 more rebels were killed near St Andrew's Hall (gunfire being more powerful than arrows), and by sunset Warwick had control of the city. The rebels were secure in Mousehold, and it seemed to be stalemate. The following day though, there was more fighting, and Kett's rebels damaged Cow Tower.

On 26 August 1,100 German mercenaries arrived to bolster Warwick's army. And then came the Battle of Dussindale on 27 August. Kett's rebels had heard the old prophecy:

> The country gnoffes, Hob, Dick, and Hick,
> With clubs and clouted shoon,
> Shall fill up Dussin dale with blood
> Of slaughtered bodies soon.

They thought it meant they would win – but it was actually the reverse. Kett was worried when a snake leapt out of a tree into his wife's bosom, and thought it a bad omen. They left the camp in darkness to fight on open ground – a tactical error. Warwick offered a pardon to all bar the leaders of the rebels, and was rejected. The battle began in earnest; 3,000 of Kett's men were killed, whereas Warwick lost only 250 men and seven gentlemen. Warwick rode out to pardon Kett's men personally; meanwhile, Kett had fled. Kett was captured the next day in a barn at Swannington, and the man who found him was awarded 20 shillings by the privy council in February 1550.

The rebel leaders were hung, drawn and quartered and their body parts placed on display round the city. Three hundred more rebels were killed, until Warwick reminded the gentry that if they continued they would have to work their own land, and the killing stopped.

Wymondham Abbey, where Kett's brother William was hanged from the west tower (shown left). *(Photograph by author)*

Robert and William Kett were taken to the Tower of London and imprisoned there. They were found guilty of treason on 29 November and were sentenced to be hanged at Tyburn and disembowelled while still alive. Then it was decided to execute them in Norfolk, so they were taken back to Norwich and imprisoned in the Guildhall on 1 December. William Kett was hanged from the west tower of Wymondham Abbey (though several of the congregation murmured about God's church being used as a place of execution).

Robert Kett was drawn up alive from the ground and hanged from the walls at Norwich Castle on 7 December 1549. As the chronicler Neville put it:

> Kett had chains put upon him and with a rope about his neck was drawn alive from the ground up to the gibbet placed upon the top of the castle, and there hanged for a continual memory of so great a villainy, until that unhappy and heavy body (through putrification consuming) shall fall down at length.

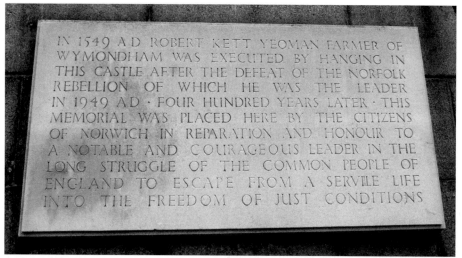

Plaque to Robert Kett at the castle. *(Photograph by author)*

His body was left hanging from the castle in the gibbet until summer as a warning. In January 1550 Kett's property was confiscated, and in the summer (after complaints from citizens about the smell of the body) he was finally buried in an unmarked grave.

The city records say that 27 August was to become a day of thanksgiving; all shops were to be shut, and all citizens were to go to their parish church at 7am and pray for God and the king in remembrance of their deliverance. The practice continued for over 100 years, and even as late as 1728 there was a festival to celebrate Kett's defeat.

But by 1949 the general population's view of Kett had changed. He was no longer seen as a rebel and a traitor, and a commemorative plaque was put on the castle walls 'in reparation and honour to a notable and courageous leader in the long struggle of the common people of England to escape from a servile life into the freedom of just conditions'.

TWENTY

Horatio Nelson

Admiral Horatio Nelson. *(Photograph by kind permission of Norwich Castle Museum and Art Gallery)*

Admiral Horatio Nelson is Britain's best-known naval hero. At 5ft 6in he was only small, but his bravery was never in dispute, and his quick thinking won him victory after victory at sea.

He was born on 29 September 1758 at Burnham Thorpe, the sixth of village rector Edmund Nelson's 11 children. When Nelson's mother Catherine died in 1767, he was sent to the Royal Grammar School at Norwich (where he may have lived either at Suckling House or at Tombland Alley) and then to the Paston school at North Walsham. Nelson was desperate to go to sea and requested his father to ask his uncle, Captain Maurice Suckling, to take him. Suckling was scathing about it:

What has poor Horatio done, who is so weak, that he above all the rest should be sent to rough it out at sea? But let him come: and the first time we go into action, a cannon-ball may knock off his head and provide for him at once.

But in 1771 Suckling gave in and took Nelson to sea. Everything was calm, so Suckling advised Nelson to join a merchant ship for a while. Nelson did so and travelled to the West Indies. He later commented that he 'came back a practical seaman with a horror of the Royal Navy'. In 1773 he heard of an expedition to see if an ice-free passage across the North Pole could be found, and he begged to go. While they were there, he went on an unauthorised expedition of his own and just about escaped from a polar bear.

In 1775 he became ill at Bomay with a high fever and was sent home to recuperate. He was depressed – but then had a vision of a shining orb and:

> ...a sudden glow of patriotism was kindled within me and presented my king and country as my patron. My mind exulted in the idea. 'Well then,' I exclaimed, 'I will be a hero and, confiding in Providence, I will brave every danger.'

Two years later Nelson passed the exam to become a lieutenant and sailed for West Indies with Captain William Locker, whose bold and aggressive tactics influenced Nelson's own naval strategies. He was promoted to captain in 1779; this was the highest level he could reach by talent alone, because higher ranks were filled strictly by order of seniority.

In 1784 Nelson commanded a frigate bound for the West Indies. However, there he enforced the Navigation Acts (which stopped US ships trading with British colonies), and this made him enemies among both the American merchants, who were breaking the law, and the authorities, whose self-interest meant they hadn't enforced the law. He wrote later that the governor of Antigua, General Sir Thomas Shirley, told him, 'Old respectable officers of high rank, long service and of a certain life are very jealous of being dictated to in their duty by young Gentlemen whose service and experience do not entitle them to it.'

He was still under strain when he visited the island of Nevis the following year and met the widow Frances Nisbet and her son Josiah. He fell in love with Frances and married her in 1787, then travelled back to Burnham. He had no commission and had to live on half pay for the next five years, knowing that there was 'a prejudice at the Admiralty evidently against me, which I can neither guess at, nor in the least account for'.

Then war with France loomed, and in 1793 Nelson was in command of the gunship *Agamemnon* to blockade the French army at Toulon. He took his stepson Josiah (then aged 12) to sea with him. When he was sent to Naples for reinforcements he met Sir William Hamilton and his wife Emma – and was immediately charmed by Emma Hamilton. In July 1794 an enemy shot blew stones into his face, and he lost the sight of his right eye. He was unhappy with Vice-Admiral William Hotham's cautiousness and wrote to his wife, 'My disposition can't bear tame and slow measures.' So he decided to blockade Genoa, which was nominally neutral but was controlled by the French. Although he knew he was in danger of the government disowning him, he believed that 'political courage in an officer abroad is as highly necessary as military courage'. In 1796 commander-in-chief Sir John Jervis appointed him commodore.

Jervis led the battle of Cape St Vincent against the Spanish fleet in 1797, sailing between two Spanish squadrons and attacking them from the rear, but his ships were held up and the Spanish were threatening to attack Jervis's ships in the same way. Rear-Admiral Charles Thompson ignored Jervis's orders to tack and stop the Spanish, so Nelson moved out of line to do it himself. Before the battle was won, he boarded two Spanish ships – the first time a flag officer had led in person to take two ships bigger than this own – and said 'on the quarterdeck of a Spanish first-rate, extravagant as the story may seem, did I receive the swords of the vanquished Spaniards'. On 26 February 1797 he sent the mayor of Norwich a Spanish admiral's sword. Nelson was extremely good at publicity, and after the battle he gave interviews and sent narratives to people whom he knew would pass the information to the press. As a result he was given the order of Knight of the Bath (his choice: firstly, because he didn't have a son to inherit a baronetcy, and secondly, because it meant he could wear a star and ribbon in public) and was also promoted to rear-admiral.

By the time Nelson was sent to Tenerife, morale in the Navy was shaky, and there had been several mutinies. Nelson's crew was one of the few happy ones, because he was astute enough to know that they needed to be kept active, and he also led in person. He was also much fairer to his crew than other officers, and when the coxswain John Sykes saved his life by taking a cutlass blow meant for him, Nelson mentioned it in despatches (which wasn't normally done for a 'ratings' crewman) and got him promoted.

In Tenerife, gunshot shattered his right elbow and his arm was amputated without anaesthetic. He had to learn to write again with his other hand and went back to England in severe pain, but he was lionised in London. And everyone noted his devotion to his wife.

When Nelson had healed, he returned to the Mediterranean. At the Battle of the Nile in 1798 he took an unusual strategy by crossing the enemy line and coming inshore, then picking off the ships one by one. He blew up the 120-gun flagship *L'Orient* (thought to be the largest warship in the world at the time), sank or took 12 further ships, and the remaining four fled. The following day he wrote to his wife, 'Victory is certainly not a name strong enough for such a scene', and organised a divine service in thanks for the victory. The despatches home were lost when the messenger ship was taken, and nobody knew what was happening. Lord Spencer, the First Lord of the Admiralty, allegedly fainted when he finally heard the news of what Nelson had done.

Nelson was made Baron Nelson of the Nile and was given a hero's welcome by Emma Hamilton. Here is where Nelson's judgement started to fail him. He fell in love with Emma over the next few months and gravely misjudged the politics of the time. He'd supported Queen Maria Carolina's foreign policy; although the navy won a victory, the Neapolitan army was vanquished by the French the following week, and Nelson had to secretly evacuate the Neapolitan royal family.

His superiors ordered him to Minorca, but he refused, saying that it was more important to defend the Neapolitan royal family. The Admiralty wasn't happy, as he'd left the navy open to defeat; and they were even more annoyed that he had accepted the Dukedom of Bronte from King Ferdinand of Naples. The situation between Nelson and Emma Hamilton really parallels the story of Antony and Cleopatra here, and Nelson became a laughing stock. He wasn't at sea to intercept Napoleon when the French leader escaped from Egypt in 1799 and spent much of his time with the Hamiltons. He even had the family on board his ship when he did go to sea. He was ordered home, but wasn't allowed to take his battleship, so he travelled across Europe with the Hamiltons. Sir John Moore said, 'It is really melancholy to see a brave and good man, who has deserved well of his country, cutting so pitiful a figure.'

He landed at Great Yarmouth on 6 November 1800. There were dinners and honours all the way to London, but his *ménage à trois* with the Hamiltons had taken away people's memories of his glory days at the Nile. Emma was pregnant by him, and George III received him very coldly because of his adultery with Emma (although Nelson had separated from his wife by this time).

Nelson was promoted to vice admiral in 1801. Emma gave birth to his daughter Horatia (and there was apparently also a twin, though Nelson didn't know of this or about the daughter Emma had had 20 years before). He was delighted because he'd always wanted a child of his own. There is no doubt that Nelson really did love Emma, and he was eloquent in his letters to her: 'Now, my own dear wife, for such you are in my eyes and in the face of heaven, I can give full scope to my feelings. I love, I never did love, anyone else.'

Nelson's behaviour with the Hamiltons and the way he'd ignored his duty meant that the Admiralty didn't trust him to have a command of his own, so he was sent to the Baltic as second-in-command to Admiral Parker. Nelson wanted to ignore the Danish fleet and hit the laid-up Russian fleet at Reval, but Parker refused. At Copenhagen Nelson picked off the ships in the same way as he had done at the Nile, then ignored Parker's order to disengage as he knew the ships would have to pass across the undefeated northern defences. He said to his flag captain, 'You know, Foley, I have only one eye – and I have a right to be blind sometimes', and deliberately looked through the telescope with his blind eye. His captains copied him in disobeying the signal, and his second-in-command Rear-Admiral Thomas Graves hoisted Parker's signal so that it was invisible to the squadron, while keeping Nelson's 'close action' signal on the masthead. Nelson negotiated a cease-fire, and the Danes agreed to a truce of 14 weeks. This made the Admiralty believe in Nelson again; Parker was recalled and Nelson was back in charge.

Nelson was finally made an admiral and a viscount, and he was in command of anti-invasion forces in the English Channel. Emma knew the Admiralty were trying to keep him busy and away from her influence, so she stirred things by buying Merton House in Surrey, and he settled with her and her husband there. Lord Minto visited and commented:

> The whole establishment and way of life is such as to make me angry, as well as melancholy; but I cannot alter it, and I do not think myself obliged or at liberty to quarrel with him for his weakness...She is high in looks, but more immense than ever. She goes on cramming Nelson with trowelfuls of flattery, which he goes on taking as quietly as a child does pap. The love she makes to him is not only ridiculous, but disgusting.

However, his family accepted Emma, as they liked her far more than they had ever liked Frances.

William Hamilton died in 1803 but Nelson didn't have time to console Emma as war was declared against France again. He sailed in the *Victory* to

The Nelson Monument in Great Yarmouth.
(Photograph by author)

blockade Toulon and stop the French and Spanish fleets converging. He was there for 18 months but made sure that his ships were kept in good repair and his men had fresh food. He kept morale high by varying his cruising grounds, letting them visit between ships and letting them take part in theatricals. During this period he learned that Emma had had another daughter in 1804, who died shortly after the birth.

The French Admiral Villeneuve escaped; Nelson attempted to pursue him across the Atlantic but was unsuccessful in capturing him. He was ill, so he went on leave to Merton Place and discovered that everyone in England thought him a hero because of the way he had pursued Villeneuve.

At the Battle of Trafalgar, Nelson used the new 'telegraph' system to signal to his fleet: 'England expects that every man will do his duty.' Unfortunately, a French soldier shot him through the shoulder. The bullet went through his left lung and ended in his spine. He was carried below to the surgeon and was told that 15 enemy ships had been vanquished. He retorted that he wanted 20! His last words were, 'Now I am satisfied. Thank God, I have done my duty,' and he died at 4.30pm on 21 October 1805.

The whole nation was in mourning for him, and Blackwood spoke for everyone when he said:

A victory, such a one as has never been achieved, yesterday took place…but at such an expense, in the loss of the most gallant of men, and best of friends, as renders it to me a victory I never wished to have witnessed.

A Trafalgar Ball was held in honour of Nelson and his victory in the Grand Hall at the Assembly House in Norwich. Nelson's men brought his body home, preserved in a cask of spirits; his body lay in state at Greenwich Hospital for three days. His funeral was held in St Paul's Cathedral on 8 January 1806, and the crowd was moved most by the seamen carrying the tattered battle ensigns of the *Victory*.

Although he'd asked various people to look after Emma Hamilton, she was largely ignored after his death; she died nine years later in Calais, completely destitute. Horatia married a clergyman in Norfolk and had a large family.

In Norfolk £7,000 was collected in 1814 to raise a memorial to Nelson. It was designed by Norwich-born architect

Statue of Nelson at the Close.
(Photograph by author)

William Wilkin, and the 144ft high column is topped by a figure of Britannia looking inland towards Nelson's birthplace. The monument was set up on the Denes at Great Yarmouth, and the first stone was laid on 15 August 1817 by Colonel Wodehouse. It was looked after by James Sharman, one of Nelson's men from the *Victory* (and, legend has it, the man who carried him below decks), until he died in 1867 at the age of 81.

A marble statue of Nelson was also set up in the marketplace in Norwich in 1852 and was moved to The Close four years later.

Even today, the admiral hasn't been forgotten; on the 200th anniversary of the Battle of Trafalgar in 2005, bells were rung across the world, starting with the Nelson Cathedral at noon and followed by bells in Sydney, South Africa, Washington, Toronto and Malta, with a 20-minute special peal at St Paul's Cathedral, a parade at Trafalgar Square and a service at St Paul's. Nelson's memory will live on even longer in the Trafalgar Woods: 33 new woodlands were planted across the UK on that day, one for each ship in Nelson's fleet and the six supply ships.

TWENTY-ONE

Amelia Opie

Amelia Alderson Opie (1769–1853), *Writer, the Artist's Second Wife* by John Opie, 1761–1807. Oil on canvas. *(Image by kind permission of Chawton House Library www.chawtonhouse.org)* Chawton House Library is a research and study centre for early women's writing. Visit the website to find out about using the library and visiting the house and grounds.

In 1830 the *Edinburgh Review* rated Amelia Opie alongside Jane Austen and Maria Edgeworth as one of the major women novelists of the previous 30 years, her specialist area being 'the passions...and the exhibition of their workings'. She was popular enough to be satirised by Thomas Love Peacock in his first novel, *Headlong Hall,* as 'Miss Poppyseed...an indefatigable compiler of novels', and yet at the time of writing, Autumn 2007, she is relatively forgotten and her novels are sadly all out of print. It's time for the Belle of Norwich – as she was known because of her beauty and vivacity – to be reassessed and given her rightful place in English literature.

Amelia Opie was born Amelia Alderson on 12 November 1769 at No. 3 Snaylgate (now Calvert Street), the only child of Dr James Alderson – a hard-working physician who saw up to 500 patients per week. She was a high-spirited and impetuous child who loved bright colours and nice clothes – a love that stayed with her until late in life when she collected prisms. Her mother Mary was very strict, and some of her parenting methods would be frowned on today, such as forcing Amelia to hold frogs and beetles to stop her being scared of them. However, Mary Alderson also taught her daughter to be a philanthropist and give coins to the people in the city asylum who called out when she passed.

In Cecelia Lucy Brightwell's memoir of Opie, she says that Opie listed five things she was scared of: black beetles, frogs, skeletons, black men and madmen. The Negro who frightened Opie was Aboar, the footman of a rich merchant from Rotterdam. He liked children and came to speak to her when she was in her nurse's arms, but Opie had a tantrum and her parents were furious with her. They made her shake his hand, then told her all about slavery and the wrongs done to Negroes. She became friends with Aboar after that, and her strong anti-slavery beliefs stemmed from this time.

Opie was fascinated by the local asylum and also by women who disguised themselves as men to follow their lovers. She was captivated by the tale of William Henry Renny, a sailor whose real name was Anna Maria Real. Real's lover had left her to go to sea, so she dressed as a sailor and followed him to Russia. Although she discovered that her lover had died, she enjoyed being a sailor and remained as one for a while before returning to Britain. She stayed in Norwich with members of the Society of Friends. Opie was friendly with the same social set and visited Real, though she was shocked to see her wearing men's clothes.

Another of Opie's interests was sitting through trials at the local assizes, partly because she liked the scarlet coats and white wigs of the judges. She attended several trials, albeit not ones where the death sentence was a possibility; she enjoyed hearing the judges sum up but didn't like hearing witnesses sworn in, as she felt they sounded irreverent.

Opie's mother died on 31 December 1784 when Opie was just 15, and she became her father's housekeeper and hostess. She called herself a 'strange, inconsistent being...now walking along the Streets on the arm of a plain Quaker, now leaning on that of a volatile Viscount'. She was very keen on writing and wrote a tragedy, *Adelaide*, about a family conflict caused by a socially unequal marriage – it's tempting to look at this as a presage of what was to come – and took the lead role when it was staged in a private theatre in Norwich during January 1791. She also had a novel, *The Dangers of Coquetry*, published anonymously in two volumes in 1790.

At the time, she was part of the Norwich nonconformist set and attended the Octagon Presbyterian Chapel. Her father's family supported parliamentary reform and the repeal of the Test and Corporation Acts (which discriminated against people who weren't Church of England). She was very friendly with the Gurney family, and she also contributed 15 poems to the first three issues of the Norwich reformers' periodical *The Cabinet*.

In London she was associated with the Godwin circle, including the writer Mary Wollstonecraft, the actress Sarah Siddons and the French Girondin refugees (lawyers and intellectuals who aimed at establishing a democratic republic in France but fell from power in 1793 and were executed or fled the country). Then she met the painter John Opie, who was nine years older than herself, divorced and from a lower social class. She wrote to her friend Mrs Taylor in Norwich:

> Mr Opie, whose head and heart are so excellent as to make me forget the courseness [sic] of his voice and manners and the ugliness of his face, has been my declared lover almost ever since I came.

John Opie clearly adored her:

> Her countenance was animated, bright and beaming, her eyes soft and expressive yet full of ardour; her hair was abundant and beautiful of auburn hue, and waving in long tresses; her figure was well formed; her carriage fine; her hands, arms and feet, well shaped – and all around her and about her was the spirit of youth, joy and love.

She wasn't sure whether to marry him or not, until he told her that if she didn't want to leave her father, he would be happy for Dr Alderson to live with them. It settled the question, and they were married on 8 May 1798 at Marylebone Church. John Opie was sensitive about being a carpenter's son, so he much preferred his wife's literary and artistic friends to her fashionable ones. He became a portrait painter and encouraged her writing. In 1801 she published the novel *Father and Daughter*, a fictionalised social protest about a woman being seduced by a rake and abandoned; her father goes mad, the rake is remorseful, and the father and daughter are reconciled at death. Opie wrote to her friend Mrs Taylor about it at the point of publication:

As usual, all the *good* I saw in my work, before it was printed, is now vanished from my sight, and I remember only its faults. All the authors, of both sexes, and artists too, that are not too ignorant or full of conceit to be capable of alarm, tell me they have had the same feeling when about to receive judgement from the public.

But the public's judgement was extremely favourable, and Sir Walter Scott told her 'he had cried over it more than he ever cried over such things'. She wrote to William Hayle: 'I like to make people cry; indeed, if I do not do it, all my readers are disappointed.'

Her career went from strength to strength. In August 1802 Opie published two poetry books, which were a combination of moral sentiment and social criticism, and they were so successful that they went through six editions in nine years. Her personality won her friends, too; in 1803 the *European Magazine* praised her 'great sweetness of countenance', 'eyes beaming with intelligence and good humour', 'unaffected, affable, and engaging' manners, fascinating conversation and a singing style that 'reaches the heart'.

In 1805 she published *Adeline Mowbray, or, The Mother and Daughter* in three volumes. The heroine was based on Mary Wollstonecraft and was against sexism and female subordination within conventional marriage; she refused to marry but lived with her lover until a series of disasters made her repent. Opie needed the book to be successful as her husband wasn't making enough money to support them, despite turning to portrait painting. Like many 19th-century painters he was dogged by depression, which affected his work.

She also published many songs to music by composers such as Thomas Wright between the 1790s and 1820s, and it's thought that she wrote the first English lyrics to the Welsh song *All Through the Night*. Between 1806 and 1822 she published four collections of short stories and three novels, which made her the most respected female fiction writer of the early 1800s after Maria Edgeworth. In 1806 the *Edinburgh Review* said her work could 'reach the heart of every reader' because it linked the lives of ordinary people to those in public and political life.

Although Opie's career was successful, her personal life was marred by tragedy. John Opie died on 9 April 1807 from swelling of the brain. She was devastated and returned to Norwich to look after her father. She wrote her husband's biography, but it disappointed his colleagues; Sir James Mackintosh said it was a 'pleasing sketch', but he objected to her apologising for not stating Opie's faults. Mackintosh felt she should have stayed silent about his faults altogether, or included them and trusted his character enough for his good characteristics to cancel out the bad.

She visited London often, meeting Byron, Sheridan, Scott and Mme de Staël. In Norwich she resumed her friendship with the Gurney family, but found aspects of Quakerism difficult. She wrote to Joseph John Gurney (Elizabeth Fry's brother) that she found it hard to think about changing her dress and of addressing her numerous friends and acquaintances by their plain names and with the humbling simplicity of 'thee' and 'thou'. She also loved society and went to the Duke of Wellington's Ball in 1814. Mary Mitford said after 'about

Statue of Amelia Opie, wearing Quaker garments, in Opie Street – originally carved in wood by Z. Leon and cast in artificial stone. *(Photograph by author)*

a quarter of an hour's chat' Opie was able to forget 'her *thees* and *thous*' and was 'altogether as merry as she used to be'. But she attended Quaker services diligently from 1814 and was admitted to the Society of Friends in 1825. Her father died two months later.

As a Quaker she visited workhouses, hospitals, prisons and the poor. She was a founder member of the Norwich Ladies Association for Prison Reform (thanks to her friendship with Elizabeth Fry). She also promoted a refuge for reformed prostitutes, supported the Norwich branches of the Bible Society and the Anti-Slavery Society (formed in 1820), and in 1840 she represented Norwich at the national anti-slavery convention.

Her career, however, had to change in accordance with her religious beliefs. In 1818 she wrote to one friend that she was writing for between eight and 10 hours a day; but after she became a Quaker she had to renounce fiction, because she said that Quakers thought of it as a form of lying. She abandoned her novel *The*

Painter and his Wife and concentrated instead on poems and prose pieces in literary annuals. She told Joseph John Gurney, 'I believe simple moral tales the very best mode of instructing the young and *the poor*,' though she didn't object to reprints of her earlier fiction.

In 1832 she gave up her house in Norwich and travelled. She returned to Norwich the following year and lived in temporary accommodation at 70 St Giles Street, then travelled again through the Scottish Highlands, Belgium, Switzerland and Keswick. Between 1842 and 1846, while she was in her seventies, she looked after an elderly aunt. At the age of 79 she moved back to Norwich to a house in Castle Street and wrote to her friends, 'I am every day more charmed with my new house and home. I do so love to look at my noble trees and my castle turrets rising above them.'

In 1849 she estimated that she wrote six letters a day, plus notes. It was clearly something she loved doing, because she wrote that year to her friend Miss Emily Taylor: 'If writing were an effort to me I should not now be alive...and it might have been inserted in the bills of mortality – "dead of letter writing A. Opie".'

In 1851, aged 82, she went round the Great Exhibition at Crystal Palace in London in a wheelchair. Because of her disability, she was allowed in to the exhibition an hour early to help avoid the crowds. However, her lack of mobility didn't affect her high spirits, because when she met 88-year-old author Mary Berry in a similar wheelchair, she challenged her to a race! Berry was in turn impressed by the 'India-rubber wheels of [Opie's] chair, which made it seem to spring forward.' S.C. Hall said the same year that Opie made 'a charming picture of what goodness of heart and cheerfulness of disposition can do to make age lovely to the last'.

The following year she went to Cromer and caught a chill, though she said she was 'more enamoured of Cromer than ever'. Her health and memory had been deteriorating for the previous couple of months, and she died in Norwich at midnight on 2 December 1853. She was buried in her father's grave in the Gildengate cemetery in Norwich.

TWENTY-TWO

Matthew Parker

MATTHEW PARKER,
ARCHBISHOP OF CANTERBURY.

Matthew Parker. (Photograph by kind permission of Norwich Castle Museum and Art Gallery)

The phrase 'nosey Parker' originated from a Norwich man, Matthew Parker, who became the Archbishop of Canterbury during the reign of Elizabeth I. There are various theories as to how he got his nickname, but the most likely reason is that he was given a warrant by the Privy Council to locate and preserve documents that had been scattered after the Dissolution of the Monasteries. This involved a lot of searching – and a lot of 'nosiness' – which upset the people who owned the documents (though it should be noted that if Parker did borrow a document to be copied, he was scrupulous about returning the original).

Parker was born on 6 August 1504 in the parish of St Saviour's in Norwich. He was brought up in the parish of All Saints but was educated in St Clement's, where various clerics taught him reading, writing, singing and grammar.

In 1520 he was a student at Corpus Christi college, Cambridge (where he complained of 'no windows, no ceilings, hard fare and small beer'). He graduated in 1525 and was ordained as a priest in June 1527. He was sympathetic to Lutheranism and was present at Thomas Bilney's execution in Norwich for heresy in 1531. John Foxe claimed that Bilney converted Parker in 1527, and certainly Parker gave Foxe a testimony about Bilney and preserved some of Bilney's letters. His religious beliefs were based on the ideas that faith was more important than penance, sermons were more important than ceremony and scripture was more important than ecclesiastical authority – so he was very much a reformer.

In March 1535 Parker was appointed chaplain to Anne Boleyn. Before her execution in May 1536, she commended her daughter Elizabeth to his care. He retained royal favour, and in February 1537 he was appointed one of Henry VIII's chaplains. Meanwhile, he was the dean at a college of priests in Stoke by Clare in Suffolk. Although it was the richest of the Suffolk colleges, its finances and buildings were in a mess, and there had been cases of 'immorality' among the members. Parker reorganised it and set up lectures – as well as founding a grammar school for the local children – and he was able to start building when he had tackled the financial problems and made the revenues rise again. His reorganisation was unpopular, but Parker wasn't swayed, despite his sermons being attacked by the prior of Norwich's Austin friary.

In 1544 Parker was appointed Master of Corpus Christi college, and his reforms made people regard him as the college's second founder. He repaired the buildings and got the college's finances back on a sound footing, drawing up a model form for annual accounts and using audits to wipe out fraud and inefficiency. He also changed the statutes so that fewer than half the Fellows had to be clerics – before then, all of them had to be priests.

The following year he was elected as vice-chancellor of the university by a huge majority. This was lucky for both Oxford and Cambridge, because under the Chantries Act of 1545 they could have lost a lot of their property to the king. However, Henry VIII agreed that three Cambridge men could be the commissioners of the survey instead of his usual agents, and one of them was Parker. Parker showed that all the colleges were extremely poor…and they remained safe from the king.

His private life was rather more scandalous. At the time, priests weren't allowed to marry. Parker lived with Margaret Harleston (who came from Mattishall, near Dereham) from 1544 and married her in June 1547 – a good two years before legislation changed and clerics were allowed to marry.

In July 1549, during the course of Kett's rebellion, Parker preached against the rebels, visiting their camp twice. He advised them to submit to the city authorities for the common good – and it went down really badly. Someone shouted that Parker had been paid by the gentry to say it, and the mood turned nasty until someone else started singing the 'Te Deum' (an early traditional hymn of joy and thanksgiving, beginning 'Te Deum laudamus') in English, and Parker slipped away. He was advised to leave the city, so he rubbed his horses' hooves with green oil and pretended they were lame, to stop the rebels stealing the horses. He walked to Cringleford, then rode the rest of the way back to the safety of Cambridge. He later commissioned his secretary, Alexander Neville, to write an account of the rising – *De Furoribus Norfolciensium Ketto Duce*, translated in 1615 as *Norfolke furies, and their foyle. Under Kett, their accursed Captaine* – which was very much against the rebels and which Holinshed used as the basis for his account in his *Chronicles*.

In 1553 Parker's mother died (his father had died in 1516), and he erected a tomb to them at St Clement's Church in Colegate.

Under the reign of Mary, Queen of Scots, Parker had to resign as the Master of Corpus Christi and was also deprived of his prebend in Ely and deanery in Lincoln. He had no income at this point, and yet he was happy without the burdens of office. In letters he wrote that he 'lived as a private individual, so happy before God in my conscience' and had 'much greater and more solid enjoyments than my former busy and dangerous kind of life had ever afforded me'. From around 1558 he started collecting antiquarian books, which included the *Anglo-Saxon Chronicle* and the *Corpus Glossary* (which was the first dictionary in English).

However, in December 1558, after Elizabeth I's accession, Parker was summoned to London. Reginald Pole, the Archbishop of Canterbury, had died on the same day as Mary, Queen of Scots, so Parker knew why he was being summoned. He wrote back, saying that he wasn't able enough to do the job, and he didn't want to disappoint the queen, plus his health was poor. He was again summoned to London and again claimed he wasn't up to the job. However, he then made a tactical error by giving Nicholas Bacon (keeper of the Greal Seal) and Sir William Cecil (the queen's secretary) a list of the personal qualities he thought the new Archbishop of Canterbury needed. A list which they said he matched exactly.

He had no choice: he had to accept the job. Though actually getting him ordained was difficult, because three of the bishops needed to officiate had served under Mary and disliked Parker, so they refused to do it. Then there were problems with the ordinal itself, which hadn't been sanctioned by Parliament at the same time as the rest of the prayer book in 1559 (it was missing because of an oversight). Eventually there was a legal resolution, and Parker was secure in the job, which he held until his death. It was a far from easy task as he had to mediate between extreme Protestants (known as the Precisians – and later the Puritans) and the Catholics.

In 1561 Elizabeth I ordered that the wives of cathedral and collegiate clergy weren't allowed to reside with their husbands in the precinct. Parker argued with her and said afterwards to Robert Cecil that he regretted accepting high office; he adored his wife and referred to her as 'dearly beloved and virtuous' after her death in 1570.

Tomb of Matthew Parker's parents at St Clement's Church, Colegate. *(Photograph by author)*

There were enormous rows over vestments; although to modern eyes it seems ridiculous that there was such fuss over what people should wear, the argument actually had more to do with church discipline and conforming to the queen's authority in the church. The queen kept vacillating and didn't give Parker the backing he needed, and the strain of trying to steer a middle course took a toll on his health.

During his time as archbishop, Parker also supervised the revision of Cranmer's *Thirty-Nine Articles* (the basis of the Church of England's doctrine), which were printed in 1563 and authorised in 1571. He organised a new translation of the Bible, translating Genesis, Exodus, Matthew, Mark and most of Paul's letters himself. This was known as the Bishop's Bible and was published in 1568. It was used in the Church of England officially until the King James version of 1611; it was criticised for both its scholarship and for including some images of God. Parker avoided this problem in a second edition in 1571 by commissioning new woodcut blocks with the name of God in a Hebrew tetragrammaton.

He died a wealthy man on 17 May 1575 in Lambeth. According to the inventory of his will, he owned £2,766 10s 11d (nearly £½ million in modern money), but as the archbishop he had to do a lot of entertaining and spent a great deal of money. A report of 1573 said he spent £160 a year on the poor (the equivalent of £28,000 in modern terms) and £237 on ministerial stipends and relief for 'learned strangers', as well as the cost of repairs on churches and so on. In that same year he spent £1,300–1,400 (not far off £250,000, in modern terms) per year on food for his household; he had 100 people in his household in 1563 and had licence for 40 liveried men as well as servants.

During the Commonwealth period, the Puritan Matthew Hardy bought Lambeth Palace and wanted the lead in which Parker's bones were buried. He robbed the grave and was said to have thrown Parker's bones in a dungheap; however, after the Restoration, Parker's bones were restored to their proper resting place.

TWENTY-THREE

James Blomfield Rush

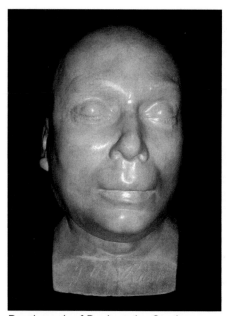

Deathmask of Rush at the Castle Museum. *(Photograph by author)*

28 November 1848 saw events that shocked the country, let alone the county: the double murder of Isaac Preston Jermy, the Recorder of Norwich, and his son Isaac Jermy Jermy. There were supplements and whole pages about the case in both local and national papers, and an incredible 2½ million copies of the gallows broadsheet were sold. Charles Dickens made a special trip to visit the scene of the murder, and Rush's waxwork was in Madame Tussaud's Chamber of Horrors for over 120 years.

James Blomfield Rush was the tenant of Home Farm, which belonged to Stanfield Hall, and acted as bailiff for the owner, the Revd George Preston. Preston had inherited it from his sister Frances Jermy (née Preston); when he died in 1837, he left the property to his eldest son, Isaac. Isaac Preston immediately cancelled his father's leases to Rush, on the grounds that they weren't made legally, then reissued them at a higher rent – which obviously didn't go down well with Rush.

There was more trouble in 1838 when Preston empowered Rush to buy Potash Farm (which was next to Stanfield Hall) for him at a sale, but told him to pay no more than £3,500. Rush bought the farm for himself, at a cost of £3,750, but then persuaded Preston to lend him the money in the form of a mortgage, which was due to be paid back with interest on 30 November 1848.

In June 1838 Isaac Preston held a sale of the furniture and effects of Stanfield Hall, but at that point his ownership of the hall was challenged by two distant relatives, Thomas Jermy and John Larner. Larner said that he was the heir through the Jermy side of the family, and also that Preston had contravened the terms of the will because he hadn't changed his surname to Jermy (which anyone inheriting the estate was meant to do), and he was selling the library (which was prohibited under the will). Isaac Preston had Larner escorted off the premises, but he stopped the auction. He quickly changed his surname to Jermy (and his son's too – Isaac Jermy Preston became Isaac Jermy Jermy); then he sold Stanfield Hall to Rush.

In August 1838 Larner distributed handbills stating his right to the estate. The following month he tried to occupy the hall twice but failed, and then arrived with 60–70 helpers and occupied the hall until the Dragoon Guards forced them out. Larner was jailed for three months and had to give an undertaking not to approach Stanfield Hall again. Under the terms of his sentence, if he went anywhere near Stanfield Hall he would be transported.

In 1840 Jermy bought Stanfield Hall back. Rush was still short of money, and when his step-father died in 1844 in a shotgun accident (in very dubious circumstances) he borrowed his mother's inheritance to stave off his creditors. Then his wife died, leaving him with nine children to look after. He engaged Emily Sandford, who was known as 'the widow Mrs James', as a governess. He promised to marry Sandford but didn't keep his promise, even though she had a child by him.

Rush was still desperate for cash, particularly after Jermy took Rush to court in 1847 for breach of contract (because Rush was behind on the rent) and was awarded damages. Plus Rush still owed Jermy the money for Potash Farm, and the due date of the loan was getting near.

Rush's mother died suddenly in August 1848 (the nurse suspected poison, but it couldn't be proved), and although she'd left her money to Rush's children he forged a codicil so he could claim the money. It wasn't enough to meet his debts, and he declared himself bankrupt. Then he started plotting with Larner, who promised Rush leases on favourable terms if he could get Stanfield Hall back for him. Their agreement was witnessed by Emily Sandford and Larner's lawyer. Rush also asked

Sandford to sign forged documents from Jermy regarding the mortgage agreement. She did so (thinking he would make good on his promise to marry her if she kept him sweet), and he hid them under the floorboards.

On 24 November Rush complained to Sandford about poachers. He went out late at night and came back with muddy clothes and boots. He also burned some papers at the weekend.

On 28 November they had tea at their usual time of 6pm; then Rush skulked off into their bedroom. He left the house at 7.30pm. Thirty minutes later, Jermy was playing cards with his family, then went outside for air (though some sources suggest that he went to relieve himself). James Watson, the butler, heard a shot (surgeon Mr Nichols pointed out at the trial that the shot left a wound around three inches in diameter, which shattered three ribs and blew away Jermy's entire heart; it also scorched Jermy's clothing, so the shooting was at point-blank range). Watson came out of the pantry and saw a gunman drop two handwritten notes on the floor; terrified, he scuttled back into the pantry and hid.

Isaac Jermy Jermy (the Recorder's son) was the next to come out to see what was going on, but the gunman shot him too, also at point blank range.

Sophia, Isaac Jermy Jermy's wife, heard the gunshot; she rushed out to find her husband lying in a pool of blood and screamed for help. The housemaid, Eliza Chestney, came running, and the intruder shot them both as they entered the lobby, wounding Miss Chestney in the hip and Mrs Jermy in the arm (she later had to have the arm amputated). Terrified, Mrs Jermy ran upstairs.

The cook, Margaret Read, said she saw Mrs Jermy running down the passage followed by a man with a long pistol; in court, she testified that he was wearing a cloak, was short and stout with a short neck, and he carried his head to one side (just like Rush did). Miss Chestney agreed – as did Watson the butler, who added that the man was masked.

They secured the outer doors, rang the alarm bell and found the notes:

> There are 7 of us here three of us outside and four of us inside the hall. All armed, as you see us two, if any of you servants offer to leave the Premises or to follow us, you will be shot Dead, therefore all of you keepe in the servants Hall and you will not take any harme; for we only come to take Possession of the Stanfield Property.
> Thos Jermy
> the Owner.

They were too terrified for the fact to sink in that Thomas Jermy was illiterate and couldn't even have signed the note, much less written it.

The groom waded across the moat and ran to Stanfield Hall farm to borrow a horse. He rode to Wymondham to raise the alarm, and the magistrate William Cann sent a telegraph to Norwich. In response, the magistrates at Norwich sent armed police to Stanfield Hall. Meanwhile, Rush returned to Potash Farm at 9.30pm. Emily Sandford had to undo the bolt and let him in, and he told her that, if anyone asked, she should say he'd only been out for 10 minutes.

At 2am police surrounded Potash Farm – and waited. At 5.45am Rush's servant Solomon Savory lit a fire; the police knocked and demanded to see Rush. When Rush came downstairs, PC Pont said, 'You must consider yourself my prisoner, on suspicion of murdering the two Mr Jermys last night.' Rush responded, 'I hope you don't suspect me of doing it.'

Police searched the farm. They found pistols (albeit not the murder weapons), a lantern, two cloaks (one of them a woman's cloak dyed black), bullets and shot. On a later search, they found a wig with false whiskers. Rush was taken to Wymondham Bridewell and then to Stanfield Hall, where Mrs Jermy identified him as the gunman.

The coroner said at the inquest that the Jermys had probably been killed by a blunderbuss, but the murder weapon hadn't yet been found. On 19 December the coroner's inquest gave a verdict of murder against Rush. He was taken to Norwich prison but claimed he was innocent and said he'd been approached by a mystery man who had obviously killed the Jermys.

The police searched Potash Farm but didn't find the blunderbuss. Colonel Oakes, the Chief Constable of the rural force, said, 'Such a search was never mounted before.' (Though it still wasn't thorough enough, and no doubt he regretted the comment later.)

Emily Sandford gave a voluntary statement in February 1849. It was said to have been written at the end of her pregnancy and signed during her first contractions.

The trial began on 29 March 1849. According to the *Norfolk Chronicle*, the court was packed to bursting, and spectators at the trial were only allowed in with an admission ticket. The trial lasted until 6 April, and if the cause of the trial wasn't sensational enough, it was added to by Rush's decision to defend himself.

There was a great deal of evidence against him. Witnesses testified to bad feeling between the Jermys and Rush and to hearing him make threats against Isaac Preston Jermy. The mortgage on Potash Farm was about to be foreclosed,

The drop used by the hangman at the castle. *(Photograph by author)*

and Jermy's death was the only thing that could stop it. Plus there were the forged documents. Rush claimed that the documents had been planted there and that the witnesses had been tampered with. He dismissed one of the witnesses as a 'shrivelled-up wretch' and said that others had been turned against him. Eliza Chestney still couldn't walk, so she was carried into court in a special chair to testify on the first day of the trial. This caused a major sensation as she had to be carried from Stanfield Hall to Norwich by teams of men in a relay. Emily Sandford was next up in the witness box and her evidence took two days. Rush cross-examined her for seven and a half hours, and it was all personal rather than related to the murder. Sandford was in tears, and the judge intervened to stop him. Rush claimed her feelings had been 'worked upon' and she retorted, 'Only by your conduct!' Sandford then confirmed that Rush had been out for two hours that night.

Rush's defence speech lasted an incredible 14 hours, but the jury's deliberation took less than 10 minutes. They found him guilty, and he was sentenced to be executed.

Rush was hanged at Norwich Castle at 12 noon on Saturday 21 April 1849, after asking Mr Pinson (the governor of the castle) if the bolt could be withdrawn while the chaplain was reading 'The grace of our Lord Jesus Christ, and the love of God, and the fellowship of the Holy Ghost, be with us, evermore.' The hangman put him under the beam, and Rush said, 'For God's sake give me rope enough. Don't be in a hurry; take your time.' Then, moving his head about, he

Rush's gravestone in the Castle Museum.
(Photograph by author)

said, 'Put the knot a little higher up, don't hurry.' The bolt withdrew, the platform fell down and the crowd applauded.

Crowds had travelled by special train to see the execution (though one was turned back at Attleborough because it was full of the 'swell mob' from London – i.e. pickpockets), and it's thought that between 12,000 and 20,000 people watched his execution. As Jermy had been president of the Life Office of Norwich Union, the whole of the staff were given the morning off to see the hanging. There was so much hysteria surrounding the execution that the authorities considered ways of making sure there weren't so many spectators in future, so from that date on, hangings were carried out at 8.00am on Monday mornings instead of noon on Saturdays.

Rush's body was left on display for an hour and then taken back into the castle so that the figure-maker Giovanni Bianchi could make a death mask, which is still on display at Norwich Castle. The phrenologist Mr Stark examined the body and reported later that Rush's skull showed great tendencies towards acquisition, aggressiveness and self-esteem. In comparison, 'cautiousness and benevolence' were small, as was hope, and 'ideality and conscientiousness' were 'very deficient'. According to Stark, Rush's perception of 'external objects and the remembrance of events' was fully developed, but his 'reflective organs' were 'exceedingly small' – he was a man who acted first and thought later.

Rush was buried within the castle grounds, and his gravestone is in the castle walls, marked simply with his initials and the date of his execution.

A month after the execution, despite the so-called thorough search, the blunderbuss was found in a muck shed at Potash Farm. The ramrod, which was missing, had been found at Stamford Hall.

Rush's children were brought up by George Soames, of their late mother's family. Emily Sandford went to Australia – the money was raised for her passage by public subscription – and married a German merchant two years later. And Stanfield Hall was finally sold out of the Jermy family in 1920.

TWENTY-FOUR

William Sheward

The case of William Sheward is one of the city's most gruesome events, known as the 'headless corpse' murder. *The Times* reported on 30 June 1851 that 'a murder of a most atrocious description has been discovered during the last week in the neighbourhood of Norwich', and the story ran and ran in the national press.

The murder actually took place on 15 June 1851, though it wasn't solved until Sheward confessed in January 1869. The discovery of the body pieces started on Saturday 21 June 1851 when Charles Johnson, the son of a Methodist clergyman, was taking his dog for a walk from Trowse to Lakenham. At Martineau Lane, Johnson's dog ran into the bushes and picked something up. Johnson thought it was 'bone or a piece of carrion' (according to *The Times* – the local reports were even more gruesome, describing the dog's find as looking like a sausage roll because the hand was so discoloured). He told the dog to drop it, but the dog refused to let go. When they got home and Johnson took a closer look, he realised it was a hand: two forefingers clenched over a thumb. So he took it to the police in a hamper and helped them search the area.

The following day Thomas Dent and his dog discovered a piece of a pelvis further down the lane. At the time, crime scenes weren't preserved, so members of the public searched for bits of the body all over the city. More body pieces were found at Hellesdon during the next five days, including a fibula at the lime kiln by PC Noller, a humerus in Lakenham by PC Wooller, a fibula in a field near Hellesdon Road by Samuel Moore of the Night Watch, and some pieces of flesh by PC John Flaxman. More pieces of flesh were discovered in gardens along Hellesdon Road by Mr Carter and Mr Cory, and one near the windmill at Hellesdon by Mr Self.

The *Norwich Mercury*, as usual, took the sensational route, describing the murderer as 'cutting and hacking his victim into pieces' and then 'prowling round the city' with his 'bloody spoil'.

On Wednesday 25 June the police dragged the river from Trowse to Lakenham. Nothing was found there, though more pieces of flesh were found in nearby fields. Most of them were the size of a man's hand; and, from the reports in the national press, it seems that various body parts were fitted together in a kind of gruesome jigsaw to prove that they came from the same source. When more body parts turned up in places that had already been searched, it was obvious that the murderer was still distributing bits of the body round the city.

John Sales was employed to clean out the city cockeys (open sewers). In June he had emptied a cockey in Bishopgate Street and saw blood there. His father carted the stuff to Bull Close and laid it out there. Constable John Sturgess was sent to inspect it and found more body parts. The weather was hot, so the body parts smelled appalling, and Police Sergeant Edward Peck had the horrible job of putting the body together in a grisly kind of jigsaw. The body parts were put in spirits of wine to preserve them and were kept in the Guildhall at Norwich. Skin and muscle were found on 28 June, and some intestines on 29 June. A thigh and part of a breast with a nipple still attached came to light on 30 June, and bones were found on 2 July.

Surgeons Donald Dalrymple, Mr Norgate and William Nichols examined the remains and decided they were human and female. They confirmed that the dissection wasn't the work of a surgeon because the handiwork was too poor. They also believed the murderer couldn't have been a butcher for the same reasons. They thought that the victim had been dead for around a fortnight. Between them, they came up with the age of 16 to 26 years (though later they changed their minds about this), and Mayor Henry Woodcock ordered that placards should be placed round the city saying that body parts had been found which were thought to belong to a murdered female aged 16–26. The placards asked for information about any recently missing females to be given to the chief constable at the police office in the Guildhall. Nobody came forward about Martha because she was 54 – and nobody thought that the medical men would be so far out in their estimations.

Another murder in Holkham in the middle of July meant that resources were diverted from the case. Meanwhile, a left foot was discovered in St Peter Southgate's churchyard on 12 July 1851. The *Norwich Mercury* claimed that the murderer watched the searchers then dumped the body parts in areas that had already been looked at; though another possibility is that the searches weren't as thorough as they would be nowadays. A left hand was found in the garden of coal merchant Mr Merry on 20 July 1851, near Southgate Church Alley; the ring finger was cut off at the second joint.

Various people came forward claiming to know or be the murderer, but they were eliminated as hoaxes. Then there was a suggestion that it was a prank by medical students who had cut up a cadaver and distributed the bits, but doctors from the Norfolk and Norwich hospital wrote to the *Norfolk Chronicle* to complain that the suggestion was an insult to their profession.

In 1856 Chief Constable Stephen English persuaded the watch committee to agree to bury the jar containing Martha's body parts in the vault, and lime was thrown on the top of the jar. Meanwhile, Sheward told everyone that his first wife went abroad in June 1851. He said she'd run off; everyone believed him because they'd been arguing for months, and she'd been heard complaining that he was unfaithful and threatening to leave him. Sheward left Tabernacle Street and rented some rooms from Mr Bird in St George's Street, but the landlord threw him out when he caught a woman staying there, and it's strongly implied that they were in a compromising position.

Sheward's brother-in-law wanted to tell Martha about an inheritance, but Sheward gave him the brush-off, saying, 'I'll tell her when I see her.' Martha's twin sister died in November 1851; Sheward didn't attend the funeral and, when asked, said he was sure Martha couldn't attend.

He moved to the Shakespeare pub in St George's, then to Lower King Street (St Peter Permountergate). He became a pawnbroker (though not a successful one – a bankruptcy notice in *The Jurist* of 4 June 1853 describes him as a pawnbroker of Norwich), and he took to drink. Finally he married Charlotte Maria Buck – the woman who had been caught in his rooms with him in St George's Street – on 13 February 1862 at the registrar's office in King Street; at the time of the marriage he described himself as a widower. They went on to have several children together.

In 1868 Sheward sold his stock to Mr Boston, the pawnbroker in Orford Hill; in the September, he moved to the Key and Castle Tavern in 105 Oak Street, where he became the landlord. But the guilt of the murder weighed on him, and he couldn't sleep; instead he paced the floor at night with a candle in his hand and drank heavily. His wife thought he was depressed; when he said he wanted to go to London and visit his sister, she thought it might cheer him up. But then he wrote to her, saying he was 'in trouble of which [she] would soon learn'.

On 1 January 1869 Sheward went into Walworth police station and told

Inspector Davis that he wanted to make a charge against himself for murdering his wife Martha in Norwich years before, and he wanted to make the charge in writing. He said he'd left home the previous Tuesday with a razor, intending to kill himself, and then handed the razor to the inspector. He had been to the steamboat by Chelsea, intending to commit suicide, but said 'the Almighty wouldn't let [him] do it'. He began to sob and asked the inspector to take everything down in writing.

Davis realised that although Sheward was distressed he was also perfectly sober – and could well be telling the truth. So he duly wrote down the confession, and Sheward signed it. Davis offered him food; Sheward said he couldn't eat, but he managed to drink some coffee, and David put him in the cells for the night.

The next morning Sheward said he remembered what he'd said and stood by it: that he had murdered his wife on 15 June 1851. When Davis asked him how or where the body had been found, Sheward pleaded, 'Oh, don't say any more; it is too horrible to talk about.' Then he added that they knew all about it at Norwich.

Martha Francis had originally been Sheward's housekeeper in Greenwich. She was 'small with golden curls', and they had married when she was 39 and he was 24. They came to Norwich in 1838 and lived in Ber Street (Sheward was the licensee of the Rose Tavern in 1842); he found work as a tailor, but when they moved to White Lion Street the business failed. They moved to Upper St Giles and he started working as a pawnbroker, but again the business failed. He placed £400 with Mr Christie, a pawnbroker in Yarmouth; he was declared bankrupt in 1849 and they moved to Richmond Hill, near Southgate Church Alley, and then to 7 Tabernacle Street, near Bishopgate Street – this is where he committed the crime.

Two days later Sheward tried to retract his confession, saying he'd made it under some kind of monomania; however, his confession seemed to fit what had happened in June 1851, except for the fact that the police and doctors thought the bones had belonged to a young woman and Sheward's wife was an older woman of 50 or 60. He was remanded in custody and put in Horsemonger Lane Gaol in London.

Inspector Davis wrote to the police in Norwich, who confirmed that a body had been found in June 1851. Sheward was taken back in front of the magistrates in London on 7 January, and they decided to return him to Norwich to face trial there.

The prisoner and escorts travelled to Norwich by train. There was a huge crowd waiting at Thorpe station, so he was handed over to the Norwich police at

Trowse, and they took him to the police station in a shuttered cab to give a deposition to the magistrates at the Guildhall. On his solicitor Mr Stanley's advice, Sheward said that he would reserve his defence. He was charged with murder and committed to the assizes.

Norwich police then faced the huge task of getting the proof together. The problem was, the murder had happened years before, and many witnesses had died or forgotten the circumstances. Medical and forensic methods of the time were limited. Even though the police ripped up floorboards at 7 Tabernacle Street, they found nothing (and they had to pay the owners £3 compensation).

On 12 January the jar in which the pieces of flesh were preserved was exhumed from the Guildhall vault. The following day the magistrates resumed examining Sheward. Martha's niece testified on 20 January, but her statement was of little use. Martha's sister Dorothy Hewitt testified that their aunt left her some money, but Sheward wouldn't tell her where Martha was. He'd simply said: 'Your sister can write to you if she pleases; she knows where you are.'

Sheward was remanded again, and the examination resumed on 25 January, with more of Martha's relatives as witnesses. They claimed that Sheward had told them nothing about Martha leaving him.

On 29 March – the day when Martha would have been 72 – Sheward was indicted at the assizes for her murder. The court was packed, and the spectators seemed surprised that a little old man, crippled by rheumatism, had committed such a gruesome crime. The witnesses told tales of where they'd found bits of flesh; and, as the local press put it, Martha was secluded from her family after the marriage and, when she disappeared, he was 39 and she was 54, 'he therefore being in the prime of life and at the zenith of his passions, she past the heyday of life and passion'.

The jury deliberated for an hour and a quarter, and decreed him guilty. Sheward's response was, 'I have nothing to say.' There were several attempts to get his sentence commuted; a petition was sent to the Home Secretary pointing out the length of time since the murder, that Sheward was now a settled family man, and the jury was from 'a class liable to be influenced by sensation'. The reports provoked two of the jurors to write to the press on behalf of the others, stating that they believed Sheward was guilty.

Letters arrived, supposedly from Martha, on 13 April, addressed from the 'City of London'. She claimed she was alive but was very ill and hoped to come to Norwich the following week if the doctor allowed her. But then Sheward confessed. He'd had a row with his wife over the money he had deposited with Mr Christie. Martha told him she would go and fetch it and, in Sheward's own words, 'with that a slight altercation occurred. I ran the razor into her throat. She never spoke after. I then covered an apron over her head and went to Yarmouth'.

The Guildhall vaults, where the remains of Martha Sheward were buried in a jar. *(Photograph courtesy of Norwich City Council)*

The following day the house was starting to smell. Sheward cut up the body and got rid of it around the city, and he did the same on the next two days. He'd boiled Martha's head in a saucepan on the fire 'to keep the stench away' and then broke it into bits, put them in a pail, scattered them around Thorpe and then emptied the rest of the pail in the cockey in Bishopgate Street. He put her hands and feet in the saucepan, hoping to boil them to pieces, and distributed more body parts around the city on the Friday. Then on the Sunday he burnt the bedlinen and her nightgown. He also made it very clear that he didn't meet his new wife, Charlotte, until '12 months after the occurrence'.

On 19 April Sheward saw Charlotte for the last time. He wrote a letter to her and their children, asking for forgiveness and apologising for 'drawing you into all this trouble and affliction'. He felt that the failure of their business was God's judgement on him for hiding his crime.

It was to be the first 'private' execution in the city (within the prison walls, with no public viewing except for some of the press). On 20 April Sheward was executed in the gaol at St Giles. He prayed with the chaplain, Revd R. Wade, for an hour, then tried to walk to the scaffold – but the rheumatic pain in his ankles was too great so he had to be carried to the room near the drop. He was pinioned and started to tremble. The press reported, 'his struggles were slight and brief', and a crowd of 2,000 waited outside to see the black flag raised, signalling that he'd been executed.

Even the gaol has gone now, replaced by the Roman Catholic cathedral in 1905. But the gruesome story of the headless body murder – and the man whose guilty conscience took him 18 years to confess – will live on in the city's history.

TWENTY-FIVE

William Smith

Black Tower, part of the old city walls next to the Butter Hills. *(Photograph by author)*

Although William Smith isn't strictly a Norwich man – he originated from over the border, in Clopton, Suffolk – he's one of the more intriguing villains in Norwich's history. His is a story involving extortion, witchcraft and treasure-hunting.

The Tudor age was the peak period of treasure-hunting; people used to dig into barrows and tumuli in the hope of finding treasure. Clearly the state couldn't allow the situation to continue unchecked – at least, not unless they got their cut, as they did a few years later with the Dissolution of the Monasteries. So in 1521 Henry VIII granted the monopoly on treasure-hunting in Norfolk and Suffolk to Lord Robert Curzon, a major landowner in the area. Curzon delegated his duties, and in March 1521 he gave a 'placard' (or licence) to William Smith of Clopton and his servant Amylyon. This meant that Smith and Amylyon could search for treasure in Curzon's name and also had the power to arrest anyone they caught seeking treasure in Norfolk and Suffolk and take legal proceedings against them.

At Easter 1521 Smith and Amylyon went to Norwich and visited schoolmaster George Dowsing in the parish of St Faith's, saying they'd heard that he was 'seen in astronomye'. Their licence apparently meant they could force people who had skill in 'raising spirits' to work for them and help them find the treasure. In the middle of the night Dowsing went with them to the Butter Hills (roughly the area between the Black Tower and Carrow Priory in Bracondale), and they dug around the area but didn't find any treasure.

Their next attempt at finding treasure was in Thorpe, an area they referred to as 'Seynt William in the Wood, by Norwich', but they remained empty-handed despite two more nights of excavations. The next move was to hold a meeting at the house of Mr Saunders in the market place, and they commanded 'Sir William', the parish priest of St Gregory's, and another priest, Sir Robert Cromer, to join them. At this meeting Dowsing apparently raised spirits in a glass, and Sir Robert Cromer also raised a spirit, which was seen by two or three people. Amylyon later said that Sir Robert held up a stone but he couldn't see anything in it, and George Dowsing 'caused to rise in a glass a little thing of the length of an inch or thereabouts'. Amylyon wasn't sure if it was a spirit or a shadow, but Dowsing claimed it was a spirit. However, they still found no treasure. At this point they gave up looking for treasure themselves and instead started extorting money from people who had claimed to be able to raise spirits.

They started with Mr Wikman of Morley Swanton, accusing him of 'digging of hilles' – he gave them 10 shillings so they wouldn't take him to Lord Curzon and prosecute him. They took a crystal from Mr White, a lime-burner in Norwich, and made him pay 12d so he 'shouldn't be put to further trouble'. John Wellys from Hunworth near Holt was next in line, and he handed over books and money to avoid the accusation of 'digging of hilles'.

Smith, however, made the mistake of trying to extort money from William Goodred, a husbandman who lived in Great Melton. On 22 April Smith, Amylyon and their accomplice Judy went to see Goodred, while he was ploughing the fields, and accused him of being a 'hill-digger'. They decided to settle the dispute at an alehouse in Melton, where they examined Goodred in the yard. Goodred denied the charge, and Smith took out his dagger. 'If you do not confess you are a hill-digger, I will thrust this dagger through your cheeks.' Goodred stood his ground and insisted he wasn't a hill-digger. Smith then asked him, 'What money will you give us to have no further trouble?' Goodred refused to give them anything. They threatened to carry him to Norwich Castle – but the row had attracted the attention of the locals drinking in the alehouse. Several large, muscular men turned out in Goodred's defence; and, clearly knowing that the charges were trumped-up, they offered to give surety of £100 (the equivalent of a staggering £34,500 in modern times) for Goodred to appear in court to answer any charges against him. Smith and his cronies refused the surety and led Goodred to Little Melton. The men from the alehouse followed them and were joined by Mr Calle, who also offered surety. Again, Smith refused, and he and Amylyon took Goodred to Norwich. Calle and the men from the alehouse followed them to the city; after another row, Smith finally agreed to take the surety.

The following day – St George's Day – Goodred came to Mr Saunders's house at the market place with his surety. 'How much money will you give us to have no further trouble?' Smith asked. 'Or else we will send you to the Castle.' Goodred again refused to give them anything, at which point Smith and his accomplices dragged him through the market place towards the castle. When he reached Cutlers' Row in the market, Goodred's nerve failed. He thought he would end up in prison for illegally trying to hunt for treasure, so he offered Smith 20 shillings. He put six shillings and sixpence down on a stall and gave sureties for the remainder. He paid the rest the following Saturday, and Smith and Amylyon acquitted him of the charge of hill-digging.

Goodred later brought a suit against them in the court of the city of Norwich. Amylyon, who had fallen out with Smith, turned witness and told the court exactly what Smith had done. The men of Great Melton went one step further, saying that they'd asked Smith if he had heard that the Duke of Buckingham (an enemy of Cardinal Wolsey) had been committed to the Tower in London. Smith's reply was, 'Yea, and therefore a very mischief and vengeance upon the heads of my lord cardinal and of my lord of Suffolk, for they are the causers thereof!' This, they knew, would be seen as treason. Especially when they added that they'd told him to be careful what he said, and Smith 'set his hands under his sides' and responded, 'By the mass, I would say it again, even if I were before my lord cardinal and my lord of Suffolk, before their faces!'

What actually happened to Smith is lost to history, but it's very likely that his alleged words were reported back to Wolsey, and Smith ended up on the gallows for treason.

TWENTY-SIX

Richard Spynk

Bull Close tower, part of the old city walls. *(Photograph by author)*

Richard Spynk is a name not often spoken in Norwich nowadays, but he had a huge impact on the city because he was largely responsible for finishing the building of the city walls.

Norwich obtained the Royal Assent to enclose the town with dykes (*cum fossis*) in 1253, and the walls began to rise in 1294. In 1297 Norwich had a murage grant (which meant the rulers could levy taxes to pay for the walls), and a second grant was given in 1305, to run for five years, followed by another in 1317. It is thought that the walls were largely completed by 1319, but there was no form of armour.

In 1337 another murage grant was obtained. It was farmed out to the merchant Richard Spynk on condition that he completed the walls. The city also granted him concessions: Spynk and his male heirs were exempt from paying taxes to the city, and he didn't have to take on any of the city offices (such as alderman or sheriff). He spent a huge amount on the walls and gave £200 and 5 shillings (the equivalent of over £25,000 in modern terms) to enlarge the ditches.

The walls were about 20ft high and 3ft thick and contained about 37,000 tons of masonry. There was also a ditch 60ft wide and 25ft deep in front of the wall. The wall ran for two and a half miles and had 12 gates at major entrances to the city. It started at the boom towers near Carrow Bridge and the first gate was Conesford Gate (also known as King Street Gate), which was the main

St Stephen's Gate. *(Photograph by author)*

entrance to the city from the south. From there, the wall went up through The Wilderness and Carrow Hill to Ber Street Gate. Then it went down Queen's Road to Brazen Doors, at the end of what is now known as All Saint's Green (the gate took its name from its brass posterns, but was also known as New Gate and Swine Gate, as it led to the old swine market). From there it went to St Stephen's Gate (also known as Nedeham Gate), which was the principal gate into the city and was rebuilt by Spynk; then through Coburg Street and Chapelfield (where there was a tower later used as part of the Drill Hall) and down to St Giles's Gate (also known as Newport Gate), which was also rebuilt by Spynk. From there the wall stretched along Grapes Hill and Duck Lane down to St Benedict's Gate (also known as Westwick Gate, again rebuilt by Spynk), along Barn Road to Heigham Gate near Oak Street (also known as Black Gate or Hellgate), through Baker's Road to St Martin's Gate (also known as Coslany Gate) which led to the Aylsham Road, then down Magpie Road to St Augustine's Gate, through to the Magdalen Gate (which was the main entrance to the city from the north and was also known as Fibriggate or Leper's Gate, the latter after the lazar house just outside the walls). From there the wall went through Bull Close Road down to Pockthorpe Gate (also known as Barre Gate) and back down to the river. The 12th gate was Bishop's Gate, built next to Bishop's Bridge.

Spynke was responsible for a lot of the work. An account in the Old Free Book of the city records, dated 1343, details the work that he had done. At King Street, he built the boom tower on the east side and supplied the two huge chains drawn between them and the machinery that tightened the chain. At Ber Street Gate, he built the portcullis, added the bars and chains, and covered the gate with timber, board and lead; on the lower tower, he built a solar of timber, board and lead, and on the higher tower he added a two-storey solar. He rebuilt St Stephen's Gate and added 'at the two towers two solars of timber, and board, and two above of timber, board and lead'.

He also rebuilt St Giles's Gate, St Benedict's Gate and Heigham Gate; at the latter, he covered the tower roof with lead and made the windows in the gates and towers. He rebuilt St Martin's Gate as well as 45 rods (247.5 yards or a little over 226 metres) of the wall between there and Magdalen Gate. Magdalen Gate had been left uncompleted ('at the level of the vault'), so Spynk finished off the building work there. He also added the portcullis and covered the gate with timber, board and lead, as well as putting bars and chains at the entrance. He paid for the cost of the gate at Bishop's Gate, the three stone arches on the bridge and the drawbridge, and bars and chains for the gate. Before then, the bridge's defence was said to be just a bar and chain.

Spynk also sorted out the city defences, which included:

- Thirty espringolds to cast stones with (kept at different gates and towers)
- A hundred gogions (balls of stone) locked up in a box
- A box with ropes and accoutrements
- Four great arblasters (crossbows), along with 100 gogions for each
- Two pairs of grapples (which were used to bring the bows to the correct tension)
- More gogions (use unspecified)
- Armour

He offered another £100 to help continue the work, if others would raise the same sum. But when nobody offered, he did the work anyway.

Clearly Richard Spynk was a public-spirited man who believed in giving back to the community. However, shortly after the work was done, in 1346, he ended up in a huge row with Thomas de Lisle, who had become the bishop of Ely in 1345.

On 20 August 1346 Spynk complained that de Lisle's men stole 10 oxen, 15 cows and 260 sheep (worth £20 and 40 marks – a total of £46) and goods worth £700. In September Spynk complained again, saying that de Lisle's men were besieging him; because he couldn't go to market, he'd lost £700 in profit. De Lisle's men also stole £260-worth of goods and beat up Spynk's servants so they couldn't work 'for a great time'. In December Spynk complained that although the king had taken him into protection, de Lisle's men were still attacking him. Finally, in 1348, he put a petition in front of the King's Council in Parliament – the highest court of appeal from the chancery court.

Bishop's Bridge, fortified by Richard Spynk. *(Photograph by author)*

In return, Thomas de Lisle claimed that Spynk and his brother William were born on his manor in Doddington, Cambridgeshire. He stated they were his villeins (tenants of his manor and therefore not free to leave the manor) and claimed *excepcio villenagii* – this was 'exception of villeinage' and meant that the Spynks weren't allowed to bring a lawsuit against him. De Lisle said that the Spynks were suing him in Norfolk to get their liberty and also 'maliciously feigning' that he was besieging them in Norwich. In addition he wanted all their oyers and terminers revoked. (Oyers and terminers were commissions issued to the travelling assize judges, read out at the beginning of each assize – they instructed the judge to hear [oyer] and determine [terminer] each case.) The council refused to revoke the oyers and terminers, and they listened to what Spynke had to say. Spynke said that he was known in Norfolk as a free man 'from time without memory', but because of de Lisle he didn't dare go outside Norwich city walls. This meant he couldn't sell merchandise or do ordinary business, and as a result he had lost much money (which he estimated at £1,000 – over £450,000 in modern terms). He didn't dare go into Cambridgeshire because de Lisle's men had threatened his life, and he didn't dare to go to Thetford, where the case was heard, so he had to pursue the case through his

An engraving of Bishop's Bridge, published by Thomas Kitson in 1815.
(Photograph by author)

friends. The court seemed to come down on the side of de Lisle. They ruled that the issue of Spynk's birth should be tried in Cambridgeshire and also said that the charge of harassment was not true.

However, de Lisle didn't pursue the matter through the courts. Instead he let the case drag on for another four years before taking it to be arbitrated by Robert de Ufford, the Earl of Suffolk, in May 1352. De Lisle then agreed that 'by reason of the good behaviour and humility of the said Richard' he would give up all his actions and demands. Clearly money changed hands to buy Spynk's freedom, as there is a reference to 'manumission Ricardi Spynk' in the priory register at Ely.

So was de Lisle innocent or not? Later he was accused by other people of kidnapping, extortion, arson and theft. He burned down houses belonging to Blanche, Lady de Wake, who was the king's cousin; he was also involved in the murder of her servant. Edward III confiscated de Lisle's temporalities (his possessions in the church), and de Lisle spent the last five years of his life at the papal court in Avignon trying to get them back.

Richard Spynk died on 30 July 1384 leaving a widow, Cecily, and a son, John. And although most of the city gates were pulled down in the late 18th century (with additions for the Inner Ring Road in the 20th century), the ruins are still there as his legacy.

TWENTY-SEVEN

Thomas Tawell

Bust of Thomas Tawell in Tawell House at the Norfolk and Norwich Association for the Blind. *(Photograph by author)*

Thomas Tawell made a huge difference to a community of the city he felt had been largely ignored: the blind.

He was born in Wymondham in 1763, the son of draper Henry Tawell. Henry died when Tawell was 10, leaving his son most of his property, and Tawell was brought up by his uncle and guardian Thomas Colman, a Norwich ironmonger who lived at 20 Hog Hill (modern-day Orford Hill).

By 1804 Tawell was living in the Upper Close, Norwich. He had been affected by blindness, although there is no record to explain whether his blindness was caused by an accident or illness. He wrote a letter to the *Norfolk Chronicle*, published on 1 December 1804, saying that he wanted to establish an Institution for the benefit of the Indigent Blind in Norfolk and Norwich. He wanted the institution to be a hospital for the old and a school for the young. He praised the generosity of Norfolk people but said:

> While comfortable asylums for old age, for want, and for sickness, everywhere surround you, one class of the afflicted has hitherto but little attracted your notice, and, probably for that reason only, has hitherto received no portion of your bounty. The persons to whom I attest are the *Blind*.

Tawell pointed out that blind people couldn't do the 'tasks of mind and body to which their talents or their industry might prompt them', and had to rely on 'the uncertain care and attention of others' for 'even the bare necessities of life'. He also called attention to the fact that there were societies for the instruction of the blind in London, Liverpool, Bristol and Edinburgh – and added that this meant that blind people there weren't cast out onto the streets as beggars or doomed 'to have past [sic] a life of uniform

Monument to Thomas Tawell in Norwich Cathedral. *(Photograph by author)*

dissipation or profligacy'. In his view the societies 'doubled their value of life' to blind people, and he wanted to establish one in Norwich.

A public meeting was held at the Guildhall on 17 January 1805, chaired by mayor James Marsh. Tawell made a speech there:

There are few present I dare say, Mr Mayor, who are not fully aware of the circumstances under which I have laboured, with regard to my loss of sight; and I hope I shall have credit for it when I say, that none can possible feel more sensibly than I do, for the miseries of all those whom it hath pleased God should be afflicted in the same unhappy manner.

He added, 'The pity that we must all feel for the indigent part of our fellow creatures labouring under so sore distress as the sloth and melancholy of a total blindness is beyond my power of words to express.'

Tawell said that the treatment of the aged blind by the asylums was terrible and explained that their basic attitude was 'as you are so old that we cannot teach you with a view to your helping yourself, our Charity extends no further and we can do nothing for you'. But he had a solution: he had bought a large house and 3.5 acres in Magdalen Street (formerly belonging to Thomas Havers and lived in by the Rt Hon. Lord Bradford) and wanted to set up an institution there.

The rules for the aged were that:

- They had to be over the age of 65
- They should not have been in the workhouse or have 'constantly received parochial relief' for the previous year
- They must not have been a beggar or 'wandering minstrel'
- They had to bring a 'complete Suit of Apparel' and a bed and contribute a guinea towards funeral expenses

The rules for the young, who could be kept in the institution for three years, were that:

- They had to be aged 12 or over
- If they were chargeable to the parish, then the parish had to give them a weekly allowance
- Someone in Norwich had to agree to take the person back if they had been 'sufficiently instructed' or thrown out for misconduct, and they also had to agree to pay any burial fees

The institution began with a committee of 16 people, including Tawell himself and the Gurney brothers. By the end of 1805 250 had subscribed or made gifts. There were also offers of help such as hair cutting, matron and medical services. They appointed a basketmaker to teach the blind how to weave, and the first formal occupants arrived on 14 October.

Tawell continued to work with the institution over the next 15 years. A committee meeting was held at his house in the Close in April 1820, and he attended a meeting at the institution on 15 May. He died on 4 June 1820 at the age of 54 and was buried in the cathedral. Fittingly, his memorial is on a pillar next to the tomb of the blind bishop Richard Nix.

TWENTY-EIGHT

George Watt

George Watt has the dubious distinction of being the first prisoner to be executed in the new prison on Britannia Road, almost 11 years after the prison was opened.

His marriage to Sophia Watt had been unhappy, and after 20 years of putting up with his persistent cruelty she took out a summons for a judicial separation. The hearing was due

Norwich prison, view from Britannia Road. *(Photograph by author)*

on 22 February 1898, and Sophia was worried that he would react badly, so she left their house in Fishergate to stay with her friend Phoebe Paston on Northcote Road.

It didn't take her husband long to find her. On 10 February he came to the house, drunk. Mrs Paston sent for the police, and when Sergeant Martins arrived, Watt said he wanted Sophia to give back the money she'd taken and come back home. Then he said something to strike a chill in her: 'Your days are my days.' When Sophia refused to go home, he threatened to kill her. Sergeant Martins took him away.

At the hearing on 22 February she told the magistrates that her married life was basically 20 years of violence. She gave some examples: before Christmas, he broke her nose and she'd had to go to hospital, and more recently he'd come home in a bad mood, kicked her out of bed and blacked her eyes. Her sons, 23-year-old James and 17-year-old Joseph, backed her story. Watt admitted that he'd assaulted his wife but claimed that he was drunk and didn't use his fists.

He said she had a sharp tongue and she'd broken an umbrella over his head before now. He made it clear he most definitely didn't want a separation. Sophia still did, and explained that she didn't want any money, but she wanted custody of their children (the two youngest were aged 6 and 9; the 12-year-old wasn't mentioned at the hearing). The magistrates gave her a separation order because of Watt's behaviour, and despite the fact she didn't want any money they ordered Watt to pay 5 shillings a week in maintenance for the children and costs of 12 6d.

Watt moved into lodgings, and Sophia meanwhile found a new home in Campling's Yard off St Saviour's Lane. Despite the fact that Watt was meant to stay away from her, he turned up at the new house on 26 February and hit her. Joseph threw him out, and Watt was up before the magistrates again. They fined him 5s for breaching the separation order and told him that next time they would deal with him severely.

Two days later he was back at Sophia's. He asked her to withdraw the summons for assault; when she refused, he attacked her with a knife. James – a Marine – tried to protect her and was wounded. Watt yelled that he would 'do for her' even if he had to wait for 20 years.

In front of the magistrates he said that he was sorry, but he'd been drunk and couldn't remember what happened. James – the only one of Sophia's five children who wasn't Watt's – had used rather more force than necessary to defend his mother and had beaten up the older man. Because Watt had a bandaged head and had clearly taken a dose of his own medicine, the magistrates took a lenient view, and he was bound over to keep the peace for six months.

In March Sophia moved again, this time to Denmark Terrace. On 23 March Watt persuaded his friend Mr Phillips to write to her and ask her to take him back, saying, 'How I think of your kindness to me. A good wife and mother. May God bless you for it.' He also asked the boys to forgive him and promised Sophia he would never drink again and would never lift another finger to harm her. Privately he told Phillips that if she didn't take him back, she would be making an orphan of the children; Phillips assumed he meant he would kill himself and had no idea that Watt was considering the murder of his wife. Sophia, having heard Watt's promises before, refused to believe a word of it and wouldn't take him back.

On 4 April Watt was out of work and didn't have enough money for food. He wrote to her that he hadn't 'had above a pennyworth of bread a day to this last fortnight and some days none'. However, despite being starving, he managed to pay eight shillings for a revolver and cartridges. Five days later,he took the gun back to the smith and said it wouldn't revolve properly. The gunsmith fixed it and returned the revolver to him.

Sophia was hanging out the washing in the back garden at 2.30pm on 14 April when Watt came into the yard. Their young daughter ran indoors, and Sophia told Watt that his daughter was afraid of him. Watt said he wouldn't hurt their daughter and, yet again, asked her to take him back. She refused, saying she wouldn't have anything to do with him because she'd heard his promises too often. Watt drew the revolver and shot her through the heart. Then he stooped over her, shot her twice in the head and battered her head with the butt of the pistol. Neighbour Emma Girling saw him put the muzzle of the gun in his mouth then take it out again; meanwhile, neighbour George Drake yelled for help. Watt immediately stopped hitting Sophia, leaped over the fence and ran across the field. Drake followed him until Watt threatened him with the revolver, and then sensibly backed off. Watt ran into the Norfolk Arms pub; two policemen arrived outside in a cab, but he escaped onto Mousehold Heath.

Dr Charles Duff arrived at Denmark Terrace and took Sophia's body into the house. He performed a post mortem and said she had been shot by three bullets to her heart and brain, which would have been fatal instantly. An hour and a half after the murder, the *Eastern Evening News* produced a paper headlined *Shocking crime at Sprowston*.

Watt changed his clothes at his brother's house, then went to the home of his friend Eliza Chamberlain. She refused to let him in, as she'd already heard of the murder. Instead, she locked the door and asked what he'd done. He replied: 'What I intended to do for months past.' Realising that she wouldn't let him in, he went to the Hope Brewery pub in St Saviour's Lane for a drink. Two customers walked him into Magdalen Street and gave him up to Constable Walter Grimes, with a crowd applauding. Inspector Flint at the Guildhall explained to Watt that he would be charged with murder. Watt said that he knew nothing about it, but he was taken to Norwich Prison. Meanwhile, the verdict of an inquest at the Norfolk Arms pub was that Watt had murdered his wife.

Sophia was buried on 18 April; there had been a public subscription to pay for the funeral cost and to help the children. Meanwhile, the police searched and found the clothes Watt was wearing at the time of the murder but not the weapon. They kept him on remand, but finally he told a friend where it was – in 'night soil' at the bottom of a garden near Denmark Terrace. Retrieving the gun must have been unpleasant, but they finally had the weapon.

During the trial on 23 June Watt said he was guilty of murder but not wilful murder. Then he made a very long statement and asked the clerk of court to read it out: he claimed a young man who wanted a pistol for 'bottle practice' but was too young to buy a gun himself asked Watt to get it for him. (It rather begs the question – had this been true, why did Watt agree to do it?) Watt said he'd 'just happened' to have the gun with him when he went to see his wife. He asked her if he could see the children, and she refused. Then he gave her a letter and said it was all the truth; she read it and told him she wouldn't have him back as her son would be angry, and she was expecting a man 'who I call my husband and he will soon put you going, so you had better be off'. According to Watt, she taunted him, saying she could have who she liked and go where she liked, and he was too late. This made Watt lose his temper and he shot her. Blaming Sophia for the murder, he said, 'I solemnly swear I did not go for the purpose of taking away her life – it was her statement that drove me to commit the rash act.' He also claimed that after he had shot her he sat in a 'closet' for a while, then walked to the city 'broken hearted' and was arrested. This was at complete odds with the other evidence.

Defence lawyer Mr Wild cross-examined Phoebe Paston and Sergeant Martins, disputing what they said and running rings round them; however, he couldn't shake Eliza Chamberlain from her story. When Wild examined James Watt, he tried to make out James had been exaggerating; James explained quietly that his father was just as bad when he was sober as when he was drunk, his mother gave Watt no provocation, and the fault was entirely his father's. The prosecutor, Mr Poyser, pointed out that if Watt had really been starving, he could have pawned or sold the revolver to buy food. He also reminded the jury of what Watt had said to Eliza Chamberlain – that he had done 'what [he] intended to do for months past'. Mr Wild claimed that Sophia's words to Watt at the end was provocation and should reduce the charge to manslaughter, citing the Reg. v Rothwell case. The judge overruled him and said that he had looked but could find no evidence that the deceased was other than a moral, chaste, good woman, and there were no grounds for the prisoner to think she was unfaithful. The jury didn't even leave the box but gave their verdict: Watt was guilty.

He was sentenced to death. Shortly before the execution, he confessed to Revd Cox, the prison chaplain, that he had bought the revolver with a view to murdering his wife. According to the report in *The Times*, Watt walked to the scaffold showing no emotion, and he was executed on 12 July.

TWENTY-NINE

St William of Norwich

The story of St William of Norwich is one of the most horrible and shameful stories in our city's history. William, being murdered, was most definitely a victim – but so too were a whole section of the townsfolk, when the 'blood libel' against the Jews was spread across the country, and eventually the Jews were kicked out of Norwich. There were one or two people who behaved honourably, but many others – including some of William's own family as well as the clergy – behaved atrociously, using it as an excuse to attack the Jews.

The legend was written up by a monk, Thomas of Monmouth, some years after the event, as *The Life and Miracles of St William*. Augustus Jessopp, a noted Victorian scholar who edited Thomas's work, said that the monk was one of those who were 'deceivers and being deceived'; M.R. James, his co-editor, was rather less kind about Thomas, basically saying he was a gullible rogue. The story was embellished still further by Thomas of Capgrave (who died in 1494) and gave rise to more claims about Jews murdering children.

William was born in 1132. M.R. James suggested that his place of birth was Haveringland, not far from the city. William's father Wenstan was a farmer, and his mother Elviva was the daughter of Wulward, a priest known for interpreting dreams. Elviva dreamed of a fish with 12 red fins taken to heaven, and Wulward interpreted it to mean that she would have a son who would become famous at the age of 12 by the 'favour of the Holy Spirit'. (Elviva did indeed have a son – and he did indeed become famous by what happened when he was 12 years old; though it's not clear whether the dream was reported before William's birth or

Detail of painted screen in Loddon Church showing St William. *(Photograph by author)*

after his death, when the prediction could be made to fit the dream more easily.) Elviva's sister Liviva also had strong connections in the local clergy, as she was married to the priest Godwin Sturt.

At the age of eight, William became apprenticed to a skinner and over the next four years gained a good reputation for his work. He visited the Jews frequently with his master, even though his uncle and grandfather forbade him to have anything to do with the Jews.

His family claimed that he was enticed away from the skinner on Monday 20 March 1144, the day after Palm Sunday, to become the scullion to the Archdeacon of Norwich. (Thomas of Monmouth's version of the story says that his mother was paid 30 pieces of silver by an unknown man – a statement clearly meant to draw parallels with Judas.) An unnamed man visited William's aunt Liviva on the Tuesday to tell her of the arrangement. Liviva told her daughter to follow the man; he took William into a Jew's house, and William was never seen alive again.

According to Thomas, the following day (Wednesday 22 March) was Passover. After dinner at the house of Eleazar William was seized, and his head was shaven. He was gagged, crowned with thorns and crucified, then boiling water was poured over his body to cleanse his wounds and stop the blood flowing. (A maidservant saw the boy through the chink of the door with just one eye – hardly likely, but Thomas believed the story. Some years later, the maidservant showed him some holes on a post in the house, claiming that this was where William was crucified. It begs the question why she didn't go to the authorities immediately; maybe she was afraid of her employer's retribution, but surely the authorities would have protected her as a valuable witness to a crime?)

The next day the Jews held a council to decide what to do with the body. However, as M.R. James pointed out, this is hardly the action of people who had planned a ritual murder, because surely they would also have planned how to dispose of the body before doing the deed. The council decided they should take the body to some remote place and leave it there. So on Good Friday three or four Jews took a sack containing William's body to Thorpe Wood. Aelward Ded, one of the townsfolk, met them on the way and asked them where they were going. He put his hand on the sack and realised it contained a body, so the Jews galloped off and hung William's body on a tree. Then they visited John de Caineto (sometimes known as John de Chesney), the sheriff of Norwich, and bribed him to keep the secret. In turn, de Caineto summoned Aelward Ded and made him swear an oath of secrecy. Aelward Ded confessed the story on his death bed, five years later, to two men who then told Thomas of Monmouth. (It's worth noting that this 'confession' was three years after de Caineto's death. Surely Ded would have confessed much earlier, had it been true – knowing that he was out of de Caineto's reach.)

In Capgrave's embellished version of the tale, that night the forester Henry de Sprowston saw a light in the sky pointing to Thorpe Wood, as did a woman called Legarda who lived in the hospital near St Mary Magdalene (the lazar house). On the Saturday morning Legarda went to see what the light could have meant and discovered the body of a boy under an oak tree, with a shaven head and thorn marks on his scalp. She went home but didn't tell anyone what she'd found. Later that morning Henry de Sprowston went to Thorpe. He met a woodcutter who said he'd found a murdered boy; de Sprowston went to look at the body, then returned home and told his family what he'd seen. He called a priest from Sprowston, and they decided they would bury the body on Monday.

Meanwhile a crowd gathered in Thorpe, viewed the body and decided that the boy had been murdered – and the murderers were the Jews. (There wasn't evidence of who murdered the boy, but clearly there was some resentment of the Jews among the townsfolk, probably due to their moneylending activities, and perhaps also some Anglo-Norman tensions thrown in.) According to Thomas, a mob wanted to invade the Jewish quarter and take revenge, and only their fear of the sheriff, John de Caineto, stopped them.

On the Monday de Sprowston and his family went to bury the body at Thorpe. They could smell the 'odour of sanctity' on the boy (a sweet, almost floral scent emanating from the body of a saint after death – in mediaeval times this, as well as a body not corrupting after death, was proof of sainthood) and buried the body without ceremony.

Godwin Sturt, William's uncle, had heard a rumour that the murdered boy was William, so he went to Thorpe to open the grave. As he drew near, the earth moved twice. (M.R. James suggested that the boy had been in some kind of cataleptic state and was still alive when he was buried.) When Godwin Sturt opened the grave, he recognised the body as William's. He removed the gag and reburied the boy without moving him to consecrated ground. He then went home and told his wife, who said she'd had a warning dream about the Jews the previous week – that they'd attacked her in the market place and broken off her right leg and carried it away. Then Elviva arrived and rushed round the town, telling everyone that the Jews had murdered her son. Again according to Thomas, the mob was furious and ready to burn down the Jewry (which was in the modern-day Haymarket area), but de Caineto warned them not to do it.

At the Synod, three weeks later, Godwin Sturt accused the Jews of murdering William and demanded justice. Bishop Eborard said, 'That which you affirm to be certain is so far clearly uncertain to us', but agreed to investigate and summoned the Jews to appear before the Synod. The Jews went to de Caineto, who told them that the bishop had no jurisdiction over them and they didn't have to go. The Jews ignored two further summonses; then, after the Synod, a message was sent to the sheriff saying that if they didn't come and purge themselves, sentence would be passed and they would be exterminated. (This was probably an empty threat, but a mob could have done a lot of damage.) The message also warned the sheriff that he shouldn't protect the Jews against God.

Godwin then accused the Jews in front of the sheriff. They said they weren't guilty and asked for a respite, but Godwin refused to listen and said he would prove it by the Judgement of God (in other words, trial by ordeal). The sheriff, expecting trouble (more from Eborard than from the people of Norwich), took the Jews within the castle bounds under his protection. The bishop realised that he was setting himself against the king and his officers on very shaky ground and he dismissed the Synod without passing judgement.

Aimar, the prior of Lewes, was at the Synod and clearly realised the possibilities for making William a saint and profiting by it. He begged for the body, but the bishop, clearly able to follow Aimar's line of thinking, refused. Eborard moved the body from Thorpe to the monks' cemetery to make sure Aimar couldn't snatch it. William's body was washed, and the thorn marks were noticed (over a month after his burial!) along with the 'odour of sanctity'. Blood was also reported to flow from the corpse's nose.

Thomas claimed that the Jews tried to bribe William's family with 10 marks (the equivalent of £6 3s 4d – or the modern equivalent of over £3,000 – the historian Blomefield puts the sum at 100 marks, or £30,000) to hush up the charges, and then he tried to bribe the bishop. But the really sensational argument was the 'blood libel'. Thomas claimed that Theobald, a converted Jew from Cambridge, said that it was the custom for Jews to sacrifice a boy at Passover, and he knew that Norwich had been chosen by lot as the place for the sacrifice that year. This was the first 'blood accusation' or 'blood libel' myth against the Jews in England; it was also repeated regarding Hugh of Lincoln in 1255. The sheriff refused to listen to the monastic claims, even though he was in debt to the Jews, and if he'd said they were guilty and abandoned them, he wouldn't have had to repay the money. De Caineto was clearly good at his job – keeping the peace and supporting justice.

Bishop Eborard retired in 1146, and Bishop Turbe succeeded him. A couple of days later, de Caineto died (this was the time when Aelward Ded could have spoken up – particularly as Turbe and de Caineto were enemies). Sir Simon de Noyers, a tenant of the cathedral priory, owed money to Eleazar, who was found murdered in 1148. The Jews knew that de Noyers was behind the murder and demanded that he should be tried. Turbe brought the counter-claim that they had murdered William first, so they should be accountable for that before anyone could be accountable for murdering Eleazar. King Stephen came to Norwich to hear the case and said it was postponed indefinitely. Thomas of Monmouth incredibly claimed this as evidence that the Jews had given a huge bribe to the king!

According to Thomas, there were plenty of miracles (though it's worth remembering that three miracles had to be performed by a saint during their life or after death before they could be canonised). A rose tree blossomed on the grave until nearly Christmas; Botilda the cook's wife was suffering a long labour until she drank water which had had a fern from William's grave steeped in it, when she safely delivered a son; and a girl from Dunwich prayed at the grave and was freed from the attentions of a fairy who kept offering to marry her.

Local miracles came thick and fast after that, including a man 'vexed by an unclean spirit' who was tied up all night beside William's tomb and then slept and was cured on waking, and a boy who was 'crooked' and brought to the tomb in a hand-barrow by his father, then went away restored after three days. Probably the most fantastic story is that of Wimarc, a woman whose husband had been taken by pirates, and she became a hostage in his stead. She went to prison with three other women; after much suffering, they decided to poison their jailer and put poison from a toad in his beer. He was suspicious and made them drink it first; the other women died, and Wimarc was at the point of death with grossly swollen limbs. The doctors she saw couldn't help her (Thomas talked about 'the deceits of medicine' – rather rich, considering what he was claiming, or this could be more anti-Semitism, as the most successful doctors in Norwich were Jews), and she visited various shrines, finally reaching Norwich. She kneeled at William's tomb, said a prayer and pressed her lips to the stone, then vomited the poisonous discharge next to it. Thomas said that 'there was enough of it to fill a vessel of the largest size', and the stench was so bad that the whole congregation left the cathedral. The poor sacrists had to clean up and put herbs everywhere.

Godwin Sturt comes in for some criticism from Thomas of Monmouth, too. He kept the gag from William's mouth and dipped it in holy water, which he sold as medicine. When one woman told him she was too poor to pay, he told her to get a hen, saying that people didn't value what they got for free. The woman asked St William to reward him as he deserved for his poor treatment of her and, the next morning, Godwin Sturt discovered that the sick woman was healed…but all his hens had died (poetic justice at its best).

So what really happened? The evidence shows that William existed, and his body was found after the murder – but that's all. The true sequence of events is unknown, and Thomas's account tends to play with time to make the story fit what he wanted it to say. He wrote the seven books about William's life over a period of several years and finished the introduction almost 30 years after William's death. As the sacristan he stood to gain much if William was canonised.

It certainly wasn't a ritual murder (and both Pope Innocent IV in 1247 and Gregory X in 1272 wrote papal letters refuting the accusation that the Jews committed ritual murder). The probability is that William's death was an accident or a murder by someone unknown, and the rest of the story grew up and became embellished over the years. Even Thomas of Monmouth admits that there were many doubters at the time – and Herbert de Losinga, the cathedral's founder, hadn't encouraged the promotion of cults. Prior Elias was set against canonising William, and Thomas had to have several visions of de Losinga – including one where de Losinga called him a 'doubting Thomas' and pinched him – before he could get William's body moved into the choir (which Thomas called the chapter house) in 1150. William's body was moved again to the martyr's chapel (the Jesus chapel) four years later. But by 1314 offerings at William's shrine had dropped away, and they were almost non-existent by the middle of the 14th century.

There isn't much iconography in Norfolk churches either: only paintings on the screens at Loddon and Litcham, and possibly a carving on the font in St Julian's Church in Norwich. There is also a screen from St John's containing a picture of William at the Victoria and Albert Museum in London. One rather theatrical personality took an interest in him: Frederick William Rolfe (aka the writer and artist 'Baron Corvo'). Rolfe wrote a rather overblown poem in 1889 called *The Boy Martyr of Norwich*; but more bizarrely, he also painted an enormous picture of St William's burial during his time as a student at St Mary's College in Oscott, near Birmingham, in the late 1880s. Oddly, each of the 150 figures in the painting had Corvo's own face…

THIRTY

The Bishops of Norwich

With our cathedral having recently celebrated the 900th anniversary of its founding, it's obvious that there have been many, many bishops over the years. Some left a more lasting legacy than others, so I've singled out three in particular – Herbert de Losinga, who founded the cathedral; Walter Lyhart, who replaced the timber roof with stone vaulting and the incredible roof bosses; and James Goldwell, who rebuilt the spire to make it the second-tallest in the country and extended the roof vaulting.

Herbert de Losinga

Herbert de Losinga was the first bishop of Norwich and was responsible for building the cathedral. He was born at Exmes in southern Normandy and was educated at the Benedictine abbey of Fécamp in Normandy, where he became prior. In about 1087 William Rufus called de Losinga to England and made him the abbot of Ramsey in Cambridgeshire. De Losinga was consecrated bishop of East Anglia in January 1091 at Thetford – and this is where the scandal comes in, because he paid the king £1,900 (the equivalent of the best part of £1 million, in modern money) for this appointment and another £1,000 to make his father the abbot at Winchester. Buying a religious post was a sin known as simony (taking its name from Simon Magus, who tried to buy spiritual powers from the Apostle Peter). However, it's worth remembering that when a bishop was appointed the king expected a gift and William Rufus had been angry that Bishop Anselm had only offered him £500.

Although de Losinga repented of his sins in 1094, William Rufus removed him from the post before he could resign. De Losinga visited Pope Urban II, who absolved him and restored him to his bishopric. As a penance, de Losinga was instructed to build churches. He obtained a licence from the king to move the see from Thetford to Norwich (tradition says this occurred in April 1094, but he was probably still in Rome at that point so it's more likely to be 1095) and began building Norwich Cathedral, planning to set up a Benedictine monastery next to it. He obtained the Cowholme meadows by the Wensum and between Conesford

Image believed to be that of Herbert de Losinga in the cathedral. *(Photograph by author)*

and Westwick by charter of the king, and land next to it by arrangement with Earl Bigod. It was unpopular with the citizens because it was next to the old market place in Tombland; the building of the cathedral meant that St Michael's Church was flattened – and to add insult to injury, the walls were fortified against the townspeople.

However, de Losinga kept a positive attitude: 'I entered on mine office disgracefully, but by the help of God's grace I shall pass out of it with credit.' He also gave much money to Norwich and East Anglia; he founded cells of his monastery at St Leonard's in Norwich and also at Aldeby, Lynn and Yarmouth. He founded a leper hospital in the north of the city (later used as Sprowston library and still known as the Lazar House), as well as building churches including St Nicholas at Yarmouth, St Margaret at Lynn, St Mary at North Elmham and St Leonard's in Norwich.

The building work did much for the city's economics. It brought work to the building trade and added to the city's reputation as a trading centre – stone was brought from Normandy, and the ships were unlikely to return empty.

De Losinga laid the foundation stone of the cathedral in 1096, and the building had proceeded far enough for the cathedral to be consecrated on 24

September 1101. Although he oversaw much of the work, he had to delegate some to his prior, Ingulf – and when he thought the prior wasn't working hard enough, de Losinga wrote to take him to task, saying how the workers were doing their job but Ingulf was 'asleep with folded hands…frost-bitten by a winter of negligence'.

Fourteen of de Losinga's sermons and 59 of his letters survive. The sermons show that he knew scripture extremely well and was an expert in allegory, making morals from every account. Reputedly, his words made the whole congregation cry in Ely. Most of his letters are to students and stressed the importance of charity. He wrote that 'the church's poor people are the Body of Christ' and 'alms extinguish sin as water does fire'. Though many of his letters to monks are rebukes, he genuinely worried about them – especially one who continually asked for leave to have his blood let (meaning that he would be entitled to eat meat and have slightly softer living in the sanatorium), and de Losinga feared that the monk was indulging his body and ruining his soul.

He was a keen reader and wrote to the abbot of Fécamp to beg him to have Suetonius transcribed as he couldn't find the book in England. However, he might not have been very good at returning books he borrowed, as a letter to the abbot of Ely makes it clear he knew that the abbot made excuses not to send a book because the binding had come undone – and because he also knew the book had been repaired and rebound, the abbot could no longer use that excuse!

Bartholomew Cotton (a monk who wrote annals about Norwich in the 14th century) says that de Losinga had a good character:

> A man endued with every sort of learning, secular as well as religious, of incomparable eloquence, handsome in his person and of bright countenance so that the generality of those who knew him not might guess he was a bishop from only looking at him.

De Losinga was clearly well thought of at court, because Henry I made him 'Clerk of the Closet' to Queen Matilda and also sent him to Rome in 1107 to negotiate with Pope Paschal. In 1116 he set off for Rome with Archbishop Ralph of Canterbury; when they reached Piacenza, he became ill and returned to Normandy. He died on 22 July 1119 and was buried before the high altar of Norwich Cathedral. The building had probably reached as far as the fifth bay of the nave when he died, and it was completed by the next bishop, Eborard.

Walter Lyhart

Walter Lyhart was the bishop of Norwich from 1446 until 1472. Like de Losinga, he left the city a lasting legacy because his work in the cathedral gave the city something absolutely unique – the stone bosses.

Lyhart was born in Cornwall and educated at Oxford, where he qualified as a Doctor of Divinity and rose to become the Provost of Oriel College. He was the

One of the Green Man bosses in the cathedral cloisters. *(Photograph by author)*

chaplain of the Duke of Suffolk, who had been embroiled in a row with the city over the New Mills in 1443. The duke clearly felt somewhat guilty about his part in it, because when Bishop Thomas Brown died in 1445, the Duke of Suffolk went straight to the Pope and asked him to give the bishopric to Lyhart. Henry VI had someone else in mind but didn't want a row with the Pope, so Lyhart was able to become bishop of Norwich without a fuss.

Lyhart was definitely a peacemaker. There had been tensions between the cathedral and the city ever since de Losinga built the cathedral and the townsfolk lost the Church of St Michael. These tensions grew far worse in 1272 when the whole of Norwich was excommunicated after a riot (although the fault seemed to be more with the prior than with the townsfolk). Trouble had flared up again over New Mills in 1443, but Lyhart managed to keep the peace between town and gown.

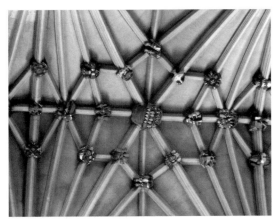

Some of the incredible bosses in the cathedral vaulting – Noah's ark is central here. *(Photograph by author)*

The king clearly appreciated Lyhart's diplomatic skills; Lyhart was appointed confessor to Margaret of Anjou, and then the king sent him to Savoy to resolve another row and persuade Pope Felix V to resign in favour of Pope Nicholas V. Lyhart was also involved in some pretty turbulent local affairs, such as calming down the row between the Pastons and the young Duke of Suffolk (his original patron's son). When Margery Paston went against her family's wishes and became betrothed to Richard Calle, the family bailiff, Lyhart again stepped in.

It was a turbulent time for the country as a whole, due to the Wars of the Roses; in addition, plague hit the city hard in 1465. But Lyhart still managed to work on the cathedral. He paved the floor of the building (which had formerly been beaten earth, damped down to prevent dust rising), and he built the west window with money left by William Alnwick, the bishop from 1426–36. When the nave roof was damaged by fire in 1463, Lyhart commissioned mason John Everard to replace the timber roof with stone vaulting and the incredible roof bosses. Unique in Europe, there are nearly 350 of the bosses, telling Biblical stories from Creation to Revelations. His rebus – of a white hart lying on its side – is visible throughout the building.

Lyhart died at his house in Hoxne, Suffolk, just before 7pm on 17 May (Whit Sunday) 1472, and is buried beneath the paving slabs of the cathedral. If you want to see his memorial to the city, simply look up next time you are in the cathedral.

James Goldwell

James Goldwell succeeded Lyhart as the bishop of Norwich. He was the one who gave the cathedral its spire, and he had an illustrious career before being appointed to Norwich. He was born in Great Chart, Kent, and was educated at All Souls College, Oxford, becoming a fellow of the college in 1441. In 1450 he was appointed the principal of St George's Hall, Oxford, and also acted as a proctor in the chancellor's court. In 1452 he became a doctor of civil law and, in the same year, he was appointed as Cardinal-Archbishop John Kemp's commissary-general. He rose still higher to become the registrar of the Order of the Garter in St George's Chapel, Windsor, and in 1460 he was secretary to Henry VI.

View of the cathedral's spire (built by Goldwell) from the cloisters. *(Photograph by author)*

James Goldwell's tomb in the cathedral. *(Photograph by author)*

He had also been studying in the church and became a doctor of canon law in 1461. Later that year he became the Archdeacon of Essex, and in 1463 he was the Dean of Salisbury. From 1467 to 1471 Goldwell was the king's proctor at the papal curia (where he obtained a dispensation for the Duke of Clarence to marry the daughter of the Earl of Warwick) and was sent on political missions by the king, including being empowered to conclude a truce with France.

In 1468 Edward IV gave him a licence to accept a bishopric from the Pope, though the licence specifically excluded Norwich. But on 16 July 1472 he became bishop of Norwich by the decree of Pope Sixtus IV and was consecrated in Rome on 4 October 1472.

Goldwell was one of the first Englishmen known to have owned a printed book – Durandus's *Rationale Divinorum*, which he bought in Hamburg while leading a mission to the kings of Denmark and Poland. In his will he left various law books to the master of the charnel, to be chained in the library at Norwich Cathedral for everyone to use.

In 1473 he obtained a papal indulgence to aid the restoration of Norwich Cathedral, which had been damaged by fire in 1463 when the spire was struck by lightning and burned down. Lyhart had already replaced the timber roof with stone vaulting on 14 bays of the nave and had left 2,200 marks (worth an incredible £2 million in today's money) for his successor to continue the work. Goldwell extended the vault over the presbytery, and his rebus of a gold well can be seen on 97 of the 132 bosses there. He also built a spire of brick encased in stone 315ft (96 metres) high, which made it the second tallest spire in England.

He retired from most public duties when Henry VII acceded the throne in 1485 – though he had been far from idle as a bishop. He had worked with both church and state, working on many commissions of the peace for both Suffolk and Norfolk. He managed to obtain a pardon for Thomas Blake, one of Clarence's associates who was accused of using necromancy against Edward IV,

Close-up of James Goldwell's tomb in the cathedral, showing the musket ball lodged there in 1643 during the Civil War. Photograph by author.

in 1477, and in 1478 he officiated at the infant marriage of Prince Richard and Anne Mowbray. He didn't neglect his duties as a bishop and carried out visitations, as well as commissioning an inquiry into cases of suspected heresy.

He died at the bishop's palace in Hoxne, Suffolk, on 15 February 1498. In his will, made the week before his death, he ordered 30 quarters of wheat to be given to the poor at his burial, a further 20 quarters the 13th day after his burial, another 20 on the 20th day after he was buried and 30 on the 30th day after. Each quarter was to be baked into 120 loaves. He also gave each of his servants six months' wages, and for every Sunday for three years after his death his executors were to give 6s 8d to 20 poor men during the period when the bell rang to summon people to mass, and they had to go to his tomb before the service, pray for his soul and stay there until the service ended.

He was buried in his chantry chapel in the cathedral – the only monument of its kind to have survived the Reformation.

The tomb also managed to survive the Civil War; according to Bishop Hall, the Puritan soldiers used the cathedral as a barracks and also practised shooting muskets there in 1643. Incredibly, there is still a musket ball lodged in the tomb.

THIRTY-ONE

The Boxers

Two of Norwich's most interesting boxers lived in the 19th century. Both were also landlords of pubs (as was John 'Licker' Pratt – also a noted bare-knuckle fighter as well as being the landlord of the Hampshire Hog).

Ned Painter

Ned Painter was one of the 19th-century bare-knuckle fighters and was immortalised in fiction as 'Ned Flatnose' in George Borrow's *Romany Rye*. He was the only person ever to beat the boxer Tom Spring, on 7 August 1818; it was a return match from earlier that year when Spring had beaten him. Ned – 12 years Spring's senior, at the age of 35 – won after 42 rounds. However, he refused another match between them, saying that they had already fought 71 rounds and that was enough. They parted as friends, and Spring claimed the title of the Heavyweight Championship of England.

In 1820 Ned became the landlord of the Sun and Anchor pub in Lobster Lane. He also set himself up as a boxing tutor and took out an advertisement in the *Norfolk Chronicle* on 1 January 1820:

> N.P. begs to inform the Amateurs of Norwich and Norfolk that he intends to give private lessons in sparring in the most scientific style and at reasonable terms at all hours of the day.

On 17 July 1820 there was a famous fight between Painter and Oliver at North Walsham (later described by George Borrow in *Romany Rye*). The stakes were £100 a side (a little over £6,200 in modern terms), and the bookies were offering odds at 5½:4 on Painter. The newspaper descriptions of the set-up are fascinating. The fight took place on a platform, and there were 100 yards of staging for the spectators, plus 60 wagons in a circle round the outer ring for people to sit in. Fifty pounds was collected at the gate and £80 more for the seating on the stage; and an incredible 20,000 people turned up to see the match. It could have ended in turmoil, but the *Norfolk Chronicle* said that 'the greatest order prevailed'. Painter was seconded by Tom Spring and won after 12 rounds. Borrow's version of events focused on the actual fighting:

> ...though Ned was not what's called a good fighter, he had a particular blow, which if he could put in he was sure to win. His right shoulder, do you see, was two inches farther back than it ought to have been, and consequently his right fist generally fell short; but if he could swing himself round, and put in a blow with that right arm, he could kill or take away the senses of anybody in the world.

Because of Painter's short arms, it was thought that he would never make it as a first-class boxer; however, although he was often beaten in matches against the boxing champions of the day, he usually managed to beat them in the return match.

After the match against Oliver, Painter's 'colours' were hoisted on the wagon and cheers greeted him everywhere, despite the fact that, as the *Norfolk Chronicle* reported, 'many of the London contingent lost heavily over the fight'. At a dinner given for him in North Walsham, Painter said this would be his last appearance in the prize ring; though he was listed frequently in the *Norfolk Chronicle* as being the seconder for other boxers and was also involved in horse racing. He was also the landlord of the White Hart by St Peter Mancroft Church – the pub generally used by the hangman – from 1823 to 1835, and he occupied the land where Thorpe station was eventually built.

In April 1843, at the age of 60, Painter was up in the dock for assaulting corn merchant Jeremiah Cross, who said he was invited to the Rising Sun Inn in June 1842 and Painter thrashed him so severely with an ash stick that Cross had been under medical treatment for 'a considerable time afterwards'. The defence said that Cross had grossly insulted Painter's daughter (which, apart from being unpleasant, wasn't a wise thing to do when her father was a noted boxer). The jury found Painter guilty; however, he was discharged in May with a fine of just one shilling, showing that although he was guilty in legal terms the jury sympathised with him.

The following month, Painter's friends rallied round. They placed an advertisement in the *Norfolk Chronicle* on 24 June:

> Ned Painter having been subjected to the expense of wanton and persecuting litigation, his friends intend giving him a benefit at the Pantheon, Royal Victoria Gardens, on which occasion the Stars of the Fancy have resolved to rally round and support an old veteran of the Prize Ring. Among the prominent professors of the Pugilistic Art who will appear are Tom Spring, Champion of England, and Ben Caunt, the modern champion.

It's fairly unlikely that Cross attended. After that, Painter is barely mentioned in the local papers, so it seems probable that he led a quiet retirement from then on.

Jem Mace

'Gipsy Jem', the heavyweight champion of England (despite weighing less than 10st and being only 5ft 9½ in tall), was born on 8 April 1831, at Beeston-next-Mileham in Norfolk, the son of blacksmith William Mace. He also has another distinction in that his may have been one of the first 'celebrity' names used as slang, i.e. 'mace' for 'face'.

He was apprenticed to a cabinetmaker in Wells at the age of 15 but was more interested in playing the violin and boxing. He exhibited his skills at fairs and race meetings, billed as 'the lad with the golden arm'. One of his first matches was against John 'Licker' Pratt, the landlord of the Hampshire Hog. Originally the fight was to have taken place on Mousehold Heath, but the police stopped it and instead they went to Drayton Brecks (nowadays part of the Royal Norwich Golf Links). The fight lasted 50 rounds, (an incredible) 2 hours 19 minutes. Mace was labelled the better fighter, but Pratt was a stone heavier and carried the day. Following that fight, Mace used to pickle his fists before fights, soaking them in horseradish and whisky. At the return match in the same place, the following year, Mace won in just eight rounds.

His first 'official' match as a professional was against a boxer called Bob 'Slasher' Slack at Mildenhall in Suffolk in 1855. Mace defeated him in nine rounds (a mere 19 minutes). He was invited to join the boxing booth of Nat Langham in London and beat Bill Thorpe in 18 rounds in 1857.

Then things went a bit awry when Mace forfeited a match twice to Mike Madden, refused to fight under the appointed referee at another match and allegedly fled at the sight of an opponent in 1858 (though, later in life, he claimed to have been beaten only twice in 500 matches). *Bell's Life* magazine described him as 'one of the most chicken-hearted men that ever pulled a shirt off'. This was untrue, and it was more likely that Mace was

Plaque to Jem Mace on the site of his former pub in Swan Lane. *(Photograph by author)*

hungover after spending the previous night drinking. But Norwich folk were angry at losing the money they'd bet on Mace. They burned down his house in Bull Close Road and were planning to burn down the pub where he was landlord – the White Swan in Swan Lane – though the police stopped them.

In 1859 things started to turn around again, when Mace beat Ned Price and Bob Travers. He became the welterweight champion in September 1860 when he beat Bob Brettle, and then in 1861 he fought Sam Hurst (the 'Staleybridge Infant') to become the champion of England. In December 1860 Mace started to run the Old King John pub in Shoreditch. He toured with various circuses in 1861, including Howes and Cushing's and Pablo Fanque's, and set up his own circuses in 1862 – he challenged people to beat him in three rounds, but nobody was ever good enough to do so.

In 1862 he fought Tom King in the last British Heavyweight Championship match under bare-knuckle rules. After 42 rounds, he won the title and the purse of 400 sovereigns. A year later he lost the title to Tom King, but reclaimed it when King retired. The committee of the Pugilistic Benevolent Association argued that the title had to be fought for, so various matches were set up – including one where Mace was arrested the evening before the bout and bound over to keep the peace.

He became an instructor at the Myrtle Street gymnasium in Liverpool in 1863, and three years later he bought the Strawberry Hotel and Grounds, West Derby Road, Liverpool. The facilities, according to his advertisement in the *Sporting Life*, included 'bowling-green, race-grounds, croquet-grounds, quoit, skittle court &c.'.

In 1869 Mace went to America. He beat Tom Allen to win the championship and then beat Coburn near New Orleans in a bout lasting an incredible 3 hours 38 minutes. He spent the next eight years travelling the world and boxing in Britain, America and Australia. In 1877 he opened a hotel in Melbourne. He also visited New Zealand and discovered the boxer Herbert Slade.

Although some of his obituaries speculated that Mace had made £250,000 over the course of his career (including £10,000 for one fight), he was declared bankrupt at Brighton in 1894. Two years later he went back to America and had a sparring match with Mike Donovan, and in

Monument to Jem Mace in the churchyard at Beeston-next-Mileham. *(Photograph by author)*

1897 in Birmingham he tied with Donovan for a 'veteran championship of the world'. By 1903 he was still wandering the world; this time he was visiting South Africa, putting on sparring demonstrations there with Jack Valentine.

His private life was as chequered as his professional life. In 1851 he married Mary Ann Barton at Thorpe, but 13 years later he started divorce proceedings, alleging her adultery. His petition was thrown out because he had a mistress himself. Despite having children by both his wife and his mistress, he then bigamously married Hannah Boorn in 1864 and had more children with her. Later, he married Alice Caroline Stokes and seems to have settled with her.

He died of 'senile decay' at Jarrow on 30 November 1910, a penniless busker. He was buried in Anfield cemetery, where his grave remained unmarked until 2002.

Mace was considered the father of the modern scientific school of pugilism. For one who led such an up-and-down life, he had strict principles in the ring, believing in straight hitting: 'Keep a straight left and you'll always be right.'

There is a monument to him in the churchyard of the village where he was born, Beeston-next-Mileham, next to his father's grave.

THIRTY-TWO

The Characters of Norwich

Norwich is known for 'doing different' – and we have had our fair share of characters over the years.

Billy Bluelight

Billy Bluelight – real name William Cullum – was one of the city's great athletes. He was born in April 1859 and was a hawker who sold his wares on the street; his favourite spot was on Gentleman's Walk outside the Royal Arcade, and he sold flowers, matches or cough drops, according to the season. He lived in Oak Street with his elderly mother.

His athletic prowess was somewhat unusual, because he used to used to challenge boat trippers to races along the river bank to Bramerton, on the outskirts of the city. He would go to Riverside Road in the morning, dressed in a striped cricket cap, a singlet and running shorts, and wearing a row of medals and he would announce:

My name is Billy Bluelight
My age is 45
I hope to get to Carrow Bridge
Before the boat arrive.

Then he would say farewell to the Yarmouth pleasure-steamer *Jenny Lind* and set off on foot. As he always beat the boat, he would wait on the landing station for the boat, where the passengers would make a collection for him. Going the other way, he would start at Bramerton, and then run across the common and

Whitlingham sewer farm to meet the boat at Crown Point, then go over Trowse Bridge and meet the boat at Carrow Bridge. The tourists in the wherries would applaud him and, more importantly, pay him.

Where he got the nickname 'Bluelight' is uncertain. It may have been from the matches he sold or it may have been associated with the Temperance movement. Ironically, although Billy was a teetaller and supported the movement, a Norwich pub was known as the Billy Bluelight in the 1990s.

The *Eastern Daily Press* reported on Tuesday 12 July 1949 that Billy had died at the age of 90 at the weekend in St James's Hospital at Shipmeadow. He had been in declining heath and bedridden for some years; in 1933 he had gone into the Woodlands

Statue of Billy Bluelight at Bramerton. *(Photograph by author)*

hospital, then moved to Shipmeadow with the other residents in 1945. In his obituary the paper quoted one of his favourite eccentricities: 'He was fond of a tall hat which he did not disdain to wear with plimsolls.'

A seat was placed at Riverside on 24 October 1949 on the bank facing the river below the road level, where Billy had met the boats, inscribed with his name and dates. In 2005 a footpath called the Wherryman's Way, leading from Norwich to Yarmouth, was dedicated to Billy, and a statue of the athlete stands by the river on the Wherryman's Way at Wood's End, Bramerton.

Robert Greene

The Elizabethan dramatist Robert Greene was very much a character, and he was also a household name for his writing. He was a very popular prose writer and was one of the first professional writers and autobiographers. He wrote several 'prodigal son' tales which are thought to have roots in his own experiences. He was the most popular writer of romantic comedy before Shakespeare, and his *The Honourable History of Friar Bacon and Friar Bungay* was the first successful romantic comedy in English. However, his personal life was very chequered, so although Greene could be considered a literary hero, he was also a bit of a villain – and possibly a victim of his own success.

His friend and fellow dramatist Thomas Nashe described him slightly scathingly as 'the *Homer* of women', but also said that Greene could write something in a day and night that would take another writer seven years, 'and glad was that printer that might be blest to pay him dear for the very dregs of his wit'. (It's worth noting that the stationers rather than the authors owned the published words in Elizabethan times.)

Greene was born in Norwich in 1558 and baptised at St George's Tombland on 11 July. He went to the free grammar school at Norwich, then took a degree at St John's College, Cambridge, in 1580 and an MA at Clare College, Cambridge, in 1583. He was also given an honorary MA from Oxford in 1588, so on the title pages of some of his works he refers to himself as '*Utruisq. Academiae in Artibus Magister*', i.e. a master of arts in both universities. His circle in London was known as the 'university wits'.

In 1585 Greene married Dolly, a woman from Lincolnshire. According to the autobiographical bits in his work, he spent all her money, then deserted her and their son after just a year for the sister of a notorious London thief.

He wrote more than 35 works between 1580 and 1592, starting with *Mamillia* in 1580. Shakespeare lifted the plot for *The Winter's Tale* from Greene's pastoral *Pandosto*, published in 1588 (though possibly written in 1585). In *Greenes groats-worth of witte*, Greene referred to Shakespeare as 'an upstart Crow, beautified with our feathers' – but it's thought that he was criticising Shakespeare more as an actor than a playwright when he continued:

> ...that with his *Tygers heart wrapt in a Players hide* [a quotation from *Henry IV part one*], supposes he is as well able to bumbast out a blanke verse as the best of you...in his owne conceit the onely Shake-scene in a countrie.

Towards the end of his life he changed the character of his writing and went from selling prose romances to writing pamphlets on sensational topics about the London underworld – telling people about the practices of card-sharps, swindlers, whores and panders, whom he referred to as 'coney-catchers'. As Greene himself put it:

> ...an author of playes and a penner of lovepamphlets, so that I soone grew famous in that qualitie, that who for that trade growne so ordinary about London as Robin Greene?

It is thought that Shakespeare may have based his ballad-selling rogue Autolycus on Greene. The Puritan Gabriel Harvey was absolutely scathing about Greene in his *Foure Letters* of 1592:

> Who in London hath not heard of his dissolute, and licentious living; his fonde disguising of a Master of Arte with ruffianly haire, unseemely apparrell, and more unseemelye Company…his fine coosening of Juglers, and finer juggling with cooseners…[his] impudent pamphletting, phantasticall interluding, and desperate libelling.

Then things started to go badly wrong for Greene. He caught a bad fever, and after his 'coney-catching' exposés of the underworld he had few friends in London – except, as he put it, at various alehouses, where they respected him because of the sheer size of his unpaid bar tab. At the time he was living in the garret of a shoemaker's house in Dowgate, London. Nashe said that Greene died from a 'banquet of Rhenish wine and pickled herring', but his death was actually caused by a bad fever. He died in London on 3 September 1592; he'd given the shoemaker a bond for £10 and left a letter to his wife on the back of it:

> Doll, I charge thee by the love of our youth and by my soul's rest that thou wilt see this man paid, for if he and his wife had not succoured me I had died in the streets. Robert Green.

Harvey also claimed that Greene persuaded the shoemaker's wife to crown him with a laurel wreath after his death. There was certainly a free-for-all after Greene's death, and his 'ghost' appeared in quite a few pamphlets. There are various woodcuts in the pamphlets, but none of them show the flamboyant author described by Thomas Nashe with long hair and a 'jolly long red beard', which was apparently never cut and was long enough to hang a jewel from.

Greene was buried in the churchyard near Bedlam on 4 September 1592.

Osbert Parsley

Osbert Parsley was one of the eight 'Singing Men' (lay clerks) in the choir at Norwich Cathedral. His position was unusual in that he was allowed to sing with the monks, despite being a lay person. He also served under both Mary, Queen of Scots, and Elizabeth I, so he sang in both English and Latin.

Not much is known about his life, but he was born around 1511 and owned a house in St Saviour's parish. He composed sacred music in both English and Latin, though his Latin compositions are considered better than his English ones. *Lamentations* (a five-part piece) and the psalm-motet *Conserva me, Domine* are his best-known works. He also wrote pieces for viols. When Elizabeth I visited the cathedral in 1578 and heard a 'Te Deum' sung, Osbert Parsley was in the choir.

Memorial to Osbert Parsley in the cathedral. *(Photograph by author)*

He died in 1585, and there is a memorial to him in the cathedral of a man playing on a harp. The memorial reads:

Osberto Parsley
Musica scientissimo
El quondam consociati
Musici posuerunt Anno 1585

Here lyes the Man whose Name in spite of Death
Renowned lives, by Blast of Golden Fame
Whose Harmony survives his vital breath
Whose Skill no Pride did Spot, his life no Blame,
Whose Low Estate was blest with quiet mind
As our Sweet Chords with Discord mixed be
Whose Life in Seventy and Four Years obtain'd
As falleth Mellow'd Apples from the tree
Whose deeds were Rules, Whose Words were Verily
Who here a singing man did spend his Days
Full fifty years in our Church Melody
His Memory Shines Bright whom thus we Praise.

George Walpole

George Walpole, the Third Earl of Orford, helped to shape Norwich physically; he contributed so much to road schemes in the city that Orford Hill was named after him. He was born in 1730 and little is known of his early life, apart from the facts that his godparents were King George II and Queen Caroline, and he went to study at Eton. In 1742 the writer Horace Walpole, George's uncle, called him 'a most charming boy, but grown excessively like his mother in the face' – which would have been a sore point with the Walpoles, as Margaret Walpole was unhappily married to George's father and

The Rt Hon. George Walpole.
(Photograph by kind permission of Norwich Castle Museum and Art Gallery)

eventually eloped with her lover Thomas Sturgess in 1734. Five years later Horace's friend John Chute said that he was 'quite astonished at [George's] sense and cleverness', but within a year Horace was worrying about the 'wild boy of nineteen'. Horace thought that Walpole's friends led him into bad ways, so he asked another friend, Horace Mann (the minister at Florence), to make friends with George Walpole while on the Grand Tour.

Walpole inherited the title in 1751 at the age of 21. His father had died in debt, and they still hadn't paid off the debts of the first Robert Walpole (the prime minister). Friends tried to persuade Walpole to marry the heiress Margaret Nicholl, to save the estate, but he refused, and she married Lord Carmarthen instead. Later Horace said that his nephew was charming, with 'the easy, genuine air of a man of quality', and 'his address and manner are the most engaging imaginable' – but Walpole didn't answer letters or keep engagements and spent most of his time drinking, having women and gaming.

As a result, Horace wrote to Horace Mann in April 1751 that his nephew was 'the most ruined young man in England'. Walpole was sometimes known as the 'mad Earl' partly because of a recurrent illness but also partly because of his escapades. In 1756 he challenged his friend Lord Rockingham to race five turkeys against five geese from Norwich to London; the winner would be the one with the most birds at Mile End and would get £500 (the equivalent of almost £50,000 nowadays). Walpole won, because he backed the turkeys – knowing that turkeys didn't roost at night and geese did. He also used to drive four deer in his phaeton; on one occasion, he was chased by a pack of hounds and only just made it into the yard of the Newmarket inn where he usually stabled the deer. He also tried to breed a very fast type of greyhound.

His mistress Patty (also known as 'Mrs Turk') was originally a maidservant at Houghton Hall, and they stayed together until her death. All his friends liked her and even Horace Walpole liked her.

In 1773 Walpole was taken ill at an inn, thought to be because of an unsuitable remedy prescribed by his groom, and became temporarily insane. Horace Walpole had to supervise his affairs; he sold Walpole's stud and sorted out his kennels, then went to Houghton Hall and found it in a mess. He wrote to Lady Ossery in despair:

> ...the two great staircases are exposed to all weathers, every room in the wings rotting with wet, the ceiling of the gallery in danger...the park half covered with nettles and weeds...a debt of above £40,000 [the equivalent of over £3.6 million in modern terms] heaped on those of my father and brother...

Horace sorted it out and got rid of the hangers-on who had stayed at Houghton, but then in December 1773 Walpole recovered his reason. He appreciated what his uncle had done and promised to be sensible. But he was back to his normal routines by March – as Horace put it, somewhat bitterly, with 'toad-eaters' round him and spending 'by handfuls and pocketfuls'.

In April 1777 Walpole's illness returned, and he was insane again. Horace had him moved to a house near London and dealt with the stewards, and by March 1778 Walpole had recovered again. He announced his intention of paying off the debts of his grandfather – but then he sold nearly 200 paintings from Houghton Hall to Catherine the Great for £40,000. Horace thought it was excessive because the debts were only about a third of the sum, and he believed that the rest of the money would go to the hangers-on. He stated, 'A madman excited by rascals has burnt his Ephesus.' Just to add insult to injury, Walpole's mother died in 1781, and most of her property reverted to him, so he hadn't needed to sell the paintings after all.

Houghton Hall, where George Walpole grew up. Photograph by Chris Brooks.

Walpole enjoyed watching ballooning, and the Revd James Woodforde wrote in his diary that he'd seen Walpole attend an event at Norwich 'in a most shabby dress'. Walpole was very popular in the county; everyone liked his manners and the way he was passionately absorbed in things. In 1791 Dr Charles Burney visited him and 'found his Lordship's head as clear, his heart as kind and his converse as pleasing as it has always been'.

However, Patty died in November 1791. Some sources say that Walpole refused to accept it and hid her body under a pile of boots in a cupboard, not wanting to be parted from her. In his grief, he developed a fever and died at Houghton on 5 December 1791. Horace Walpole inherited the title and gradually started reversing the changes his nephew had made to the hall.

In 1792 Rochester Lane (the main entrance to the Castle Ditches) was widened. The work was financed by public subscription, and Walpole had been one of the biggest subscribers. The new road, Orford Street, was named after him, and Hog Hill became Orford Hill.

THIRTY-THREE

The Doctors of Norwich

The story of the development of medicine in Norfolk and the doctors who pushed the boundaries forward could have made a whole book on its own. I have singled out five in particular – Benjamin Gooch, who helped to set up the Norfolk and Norwich hospital; Edward Rigby, who brought vaccination to the city; John Green Crosse, one of our most renowned surgeons; William Cadge, a specialist in the 'bladder stone', who helped to extend the hospital; and Sir Peter Eade, who wrote some of the first case notes about diphtheria and made sure there were plenty of green spaces in the city.

Benjamin Gooch

Benjamin Gooch was born on 11 November 1708, the son of the rector of Ashwellthorpe. He studied in London, where he was apprenticed to the surgeon Mr Symons and then to the Norwich surgeon David Amyas, then finally became apprentice to the GP Robert Bransby at Hapton. He moved to Shotesham and married Bransby's daughter Elizabeth. When Bransby died in 1748, Gooch became principal of the practice and worked as an apothecary surgeon.

Benjamin Gooch. *(Picture courtesy of the Hospital Arts Project, which looks after the historic collections of the Norwich and Norwich Hospital University Trust)*

Gooch became friendly with William Fellowes, who built a cottage hospital at Shotesham. The land for the hospital was bought in 1731 and, although it's not known when the hospital was built, Gooch worked there from at least 1754 and acquired surgical skills. His health was poor, so he wrote books to help instruct the young surgeons of the day. The first volume of his *Cases and Practical Remarks in Surgery* was published in 1758 – one of the few surgical textbooks by English surgeons in the 18th century – and the second volume was published eight years later. The book included chapters on trepanning (one case described a parson who fell off his horse and fractured his skull; Gooch trepanned his skull to let out the pus, and the parson lived for years afterwards), aneurysms, suturing and how to open a dead body. A third volume followed in 1773, dedicated to the governors of the Norfolk and Norwich Hospital: 'a testimony of the honour done me in electing me as consulting surgeon'. The book described radical operations on breast cancer and an outbreak of mumps. He also created the Gooch's splint – a splint used in treating difficult compound fractures of the leg – which was used until plaster of Paris replaced it in the treatment of fractures in the 1920s.

Gooch was the leading lithotomist (i.e. surgeon who removed stones) in the early 18th century. He was particularly skilled at operating on bladder stones, which were more common in Norfolk than anywhere else in the country. The *Norwich Gazette* of 14 July 1746 describes an operation where Gooch assisted John Harmer in removing a stone from 48-year-old gardener John Howse. This sounds relatively normal until you realise that the stone weighed over 14.5oz (400g) and measured 8in by 12in (roughly 22cm x 34cm). A week later it was reported that the patient was recovering well and out of danger.

At the time the nearest hospitals to Norwich from London were at Shotesham and Bury St Edmunds, so it was clear that a hospital was needed at Norwich. In 1758 Bishop Hayter of Norwich asked Gooch to visit the London hospitals and get information about their management and design. The architect William Ivory drew up plans for the new hospital in Norwich, but then Hayter died and nothing happened until 1770, when William Fellowes organised a meeting at the Guildhall to start a committee and subscription to build the hospital. The foundation stone was laid on 5 March 1771, and the general hospital built for the relief of the sick, the lame and the poor cost £13,323 8s 11d.

Gooch had plans for the way the hospital should be run. He wanted checked curtains that could be drawn round the bed for privacy, feather bolsters and beds stuffed with straw and adorned with two blankets and a 'coverlid'. He said that the wards shouldn't be overcrowded with beds and should be kept clean, well ventilated by opening windows, and lit with lamps 'supplied with the finest Spermacetti oil'. There were still no drains, no trained nurses, no piped water (a man was paid a shilling an hour to raise water from a well) and no anaesthetic. Before anaesthetic was introduced in the 1840s, the patients were given laudanum or made drunk to dull the pain. The first outpatient was treated at the hospital on 25 July 1771, and the first patient was admitted to the wards on 7 November 1771.

Although Gooch was appointed the consultant surgeon to the hospital, he never operated there because he was ill with kidney stones and lame after an accident. However, in 1772 he said that he had been a consulting surgeon for over 15 years, assisting some 150 surgeons and more than 20 physicians in that time.

In Autumn 1775 his health grew worse so he moved back to Halesworth to stay with his only child, Elizabeth, and her surgeon husband John D'Urban. He died on 11 February 1776.

Edward Rigby

Edward Rigby had an incredible amount of energy. As well as shouldering the full workload of a busy doctor, he continued to study throughout his life and also took a part in the city's administration, holding all the high civil offices.

He was born in Chowbent, Lancashire, on 27 December 1747, and educated at Dr Priestley's school in Warrington. In 1762 he was apprenticed to the surgeon

David Martineau, a relative of his mother's, in Norwich and afterwards studied in London. He was admitted a member of the Corporation of Surgeons on 4 May 1769 and was a specialist in gallstone removal. He was also an 'accoucher' (an obstetrician), and in 1776 he published the work that made his name: *An Essay on the Uterine Haemorrhage*. It was translated into French and German, and went into six editions in England. The *Norfolk Chronicle* later said that the book had 'been the means of saving many lives'. He also travelled; in July 1789 he visited France, and his letters describe what he called 'the most extraordinary revolution that perhaps ever took place in human society'.

Edward Rigby. *(Picture courtesy of the Hospital Arts Project, which looks after the historic collections of the Norwich and Norwich Hospital University Trust)*

In terms of the Norfolk and Norwich hospital, he became its assistant surgeon in 1771, its surgeon in 1790 and its physician in 1814. Between 1790 and 1814 he performed 106 operations to remove stones.

He was also busy in the city's administration; as the *Norfolk Chronicle* remarked in his obituary, 'his duties as a doctor, extensive as they were, did not prevent him from devoting a portion of his time to the several duties of a citizen and a magistrate while he employed his spare moments in literary and scientific pursuits'. In 1783 he became a member of the Corporation of Guardians of Norwich, and he promoted the economical administration of the Poor Laws. He was opposed to building a new workhouse and felt that home allowances were better for the poor, as well as cheaper for the city. In 1786 he helped to establish the Norfolk Benevolent Society, which helped the widows and orphans of medical practitioners. He became an alderman in 1802, the sheriff in 1803 and the chief magistrate and mayor of Norwich in 1805. During this period he presided over a meeting where a resolution was passed to halt smallpox and to introduce vaccine inoculation throughout the city.

He actually had his own smallpox hospital, as well as a licence to keep '12 lunaticks' in a house in Lakenham. He was a keen naturalist and grew herbs used for medicine on his 300-acre farm at Framingham, including opium poppies. However, he was so keen on trees that he dispossessed some of his tenants and demolished their houses to plant more. The epitaph on his tomb in Framingham Earl reads:

A monument for Rigby do you seek?
On every side the whispering woodlands speak.

In 1803 he remarried; he and his wife Anne had 12 children together, including quadruplets on 15 August 1817 (when, according to a later report in *Gentleman's Magazine*, he was a grandfather at the time). The city council gave him an inscribed silver breadbasket to mark the occasion.

He died on 27 October 1821 and was buried in the churchyard at Framingham Earl. His obituary in the *Norfolk Chronicle* said that they couldn't do justice to his character and his 'excellencies' as a husband, father, friend or 'his tender feelings which marked his medical practice'. They concluded that it was 'astonishing how he was enabled to perform so many and such arduous duties with the regularity, zeal and correctness which characterised all his action', though they believed they knew the reason why: 'he lived abstemiously and rose early'.

John Green Crosse

John Green Crosse was born on 6 September 1790 at Boyton Hall, Great Finborough, near Stowmarket. His parents wanted him to be a lawyer, but when Crosse broke his leg at the age of 14 and was treated by Thomas Bayly, the surgeon apothecary in Stowmarket, the experience made Crosse decide that he wanted to be a doctor. Just before his 16th birthday, he became apprenticed to Thomas Bayly. He kept a journal of his experiences, starting with rolling up pills and keeping the surgery tidy – as well as placing leeches in boxes, ready to be put on a patient's body. His first operation was performed on 14 September 1806, when

John Green Crosse. *(Picture courtesy of the Hospital Arts Project, which looks after the historic collections of the Norwich and Norwich Hospital University Trust)*

he drew a tooth (and noted that he performed the operation before breakfast).

At this time, trainee doctors did an apprenticeship of practical work, then studied and worked in a London hospital. In 1811 Crosse studied at St George's Hospital and at the Great Windmill Street School of Anatomy which, as well as teaching surgery and anatomy, taught physiology, pathology, midwifery and diseases of women and children. As part of his training, he spent a year 'walking the hospital' – which meant watching operations, attending ward rounds and taking case notes for the 'dressers' (the surgeon's assistants).

He became a member of the Royal College of Surgeons in 1813 and was noted for his skill in dissection. He was appointed as an assistant to James Macartney, the professor of anatomy and surgery at Trinity College in Dublin; during this period he was forced to be associated with the 'resurrection men', as the only legal source of supply of bodies for medical students to dissect were those of executed murderers. There weren't many of them, so the 'resurrection men' used to take bodies from the grave soon after burial and sell them to anatomy schools. The medical profession lobbied to be allowed to use unclaimed bodies from workhouses and hospitals, but this didn't happen until the Anatomy Act was passed in 1832.

Crosse went to Paris to study the work of Parisian hospitals and noted that he was disappointed with the lectures, except for those on medical jurisprudence. In March

Memorial window to John Green Crosse in Norwich Cathedral. *(Photograph by author)*

1815 he settled in Norwich and set up a practice in the city before marrying Thomas Bayly's daughter Dorothy the following year. They lived at No. 22 St Giles Street (now No. 45), moving to a house on Orford Hill as his family grew (the house later became the Livingstone Hotel but was pulled down for redevelopment in the 20th century).

His reputation as a surgeon grew, especially for his work in lithotomy (removing stones). One of his students timed an operation as taking 90 seconds, and Crosse himself talked of operating on a child in 3½ minutes. In 1823 he became the assistant surgeon to the Norfolk and Norwich Hospital, and in 1826 he became its surgeon. In 1833 he won the Jacksonian prize at the Royal College of Surgeons for his work on urinary calculus and was made a fellow of the Royal Society. In 1846 he was elected as one of the original 300 fellows of the Royal College of Surgeons.

As with Rigby, Crosse's apprentices all noted his enthusiasm for acquiring medical and surgical knowledge, and his untiring energy. But in 1848 Crosse's health started to fail and grew worse over the next two years. He died on 9 June 1850 and was buried in the cloisters at Norwich Cathedral. Dr Edward Copeman said of Crosse that he would have been successful at anything he did, because of his 'persevering industry and unwearied application, his determination to accomplish whatever he undertook to the best of his ability, and his undeviating punctuality and sound judgement'.

William Cadge

William Cadge was born in Hoveton in 1822 into a farming family. He studied in London at University College Hospital and qualified in 1845; he was present when Robert Liston operated in 1846 and ether was used for the first time as a general anaesthetic. He became a fellow of the Royal College of Surgeons in 1848 and was appointed the assistant surgeon at University College Hospital London, but resigned due to ill health.

In 1850 Cadge returned to Norfolk to work at a practice with Donald Dalrymple in St Giles Street and at the Norfolk and Norwich Hospital. He was elected the assistant surgeon at the hospital in 1854 and then full surgeon in 1857, before retiring from his post as surgeon in 1890. He had a reputation as a pioneering surgeon and was the last of the Norwich lithotomy specialists; Cadge operated on 240 cases at the hospital and over 140 cases in his private practice.

Like Rigby, Cadge also threw himself into the city's civic administration; he was the sheriff of Norwich in 1876 and also became a magistrate and a Trustee of the Great Hospital. He received the Freedom of the City in 1890 for his services and

William Cadge. *(Picture courtesy of the Hospital Arts Project, which looks after the historic collections of the Norwich and Norwich Hospital University Trust)*

the amount he gave towards the rebuilding of the hospital. In January 1899 *The Nursing Record and Hospital World* recorded that he gave £10,000 to the endowment fund of the hospital (the equivalent of over £¾ million nowadays) 'making £20,000 given by this gentlemen in recent years'.

He died on 25 June 1903 and was buried in St Mary's Church, Earlham. A stained-glass window to his memory was put up in the north transept of Norwich Cathedral, and surgeons from 22 different countries attended the unveiling ceremony in 1904. The *British Journal of Nursing* said that he left an estate worth just over £110,000, and in his will he left another £5,000 to the endowment fund of the hospital.

Sir Peter Eade

Peter Eade was born in Acle in 1825, the son of a doctor. The family moved to Blofield, and he was educated firstly at home, then at Yarmouth Grammar School – where he later said he was 'the most unhappy of my whole life' – and then studied medicine in London. The calendar of King's College London shows that in 1847 he practically swept the board with prizes: he obtained honours at a second examination for the degree of Bachelor of Medicine and was awarded the gold medal in physiology and comparative anatomy, the gold medal in medicine, and the gold medal and a scholarship in surgery. The *Lancet* called him 'one of the best known provincial physicians in the country'.

Churchman House, the former residence of Sir Peter Eade. *(Photograph by author)*

He returned to Norwich in 1856 and worked with his father at Blofield before obtaining a place at the city dispensary and becoming the pupil of John Green Crosse. He was the physician at the Norfolk and Norwich Hospital in 1858 until he retired in 1888. A year after his appointment as physician he had admitted various cases of 'imperfect paraplegia' and discovered that his patients had all had a sore throat five or six weeks before coming to the hospital; he realised that this was caused by diphtheria, and when he wrote in the *Lancet* about his cases, they were the first recorded cases of diphtheria. He also wrote pamphlets, was an expert in the history of the St Giles parish and reared tortoises.

Following the tradition of other medical men in the city, Eade was busy in the city's administration as well as in medicine. He became a member of the Board of Guardians in 1863 and was the first president of the Medical and Chirurgical Society in 1867. In his speech he said, 'This is an age of medical change...in spite of being engaged in the active busy pursuits of daily practice, time must be found to learn the ever new facts of medical science.'

He was caught up in the Thorpe rail accident on 10 September 1874 on his return from Lowestoft. He was thrown out of the carriage on the impact and was briefly unconscious, but as soon as he came to and realised his injuries were superficial – bruising and a few contusions – he started helping the injured passengers. He noted in his diary that he had to use broken chairs as splints and torn-up towels for bandages.

Eade moved to a house in St Giles in 1877. He was the sheriff of the city and also mayor of the city three times – in 1883, 1893 and 1895 (after Charles

Bignold died partway through his mayoral year). On 28 December 1884 he gave a dinner in St Andrew's Hall for 800 poor people over the age of 60, and for the 335 who couldn't attend he sent half a pound of tea. He also decided that a Christmas dinner was a bad idea because the cold weather and icy paths might be dangerous for the elderly, so in future mayoralties he held a dinner in the summer instead.

With the manufacturer F.W. Harmer, Eade was responsible for the laying out of Chapelfield Gardens and Castle Gardens, and the city's acquisition of Mousehold Heath. In February 1876 he wrote to the newspapers saying that recreation grounds were important in a large crowded city for 'healthy juvenile development'.

He was knighted by Queen Victoria on 1 August 1885 on the Isle of Wight, in recognition of his contribution to public services, and 10 years later he was made a Freeman of the City of Norwich. He died on 12 August 1915, aged 90; he had been ill and bedridden for three weeks, but his obituary in the *Eastern Daily Press* said that before then 'his remarkable energy and vitality enabled him to continue his normal occupation'. His biographer Sydney Long claimed: 'A more honourable man and patriotic citizen of Norwich it would be impossible to find'.

Eade was buried in Blofield, and there is also a memorial to him in St Giles Church.

THIRTY-FOUR

The Norwich Inventors

A city the size of Norwich has produced several inventors in its time. Some have faded into the mists of time – such as Mr J. Ayton, the inventor of a new type of skate called the 'tachypos', and the carpenter Samuel Rainbird, who patented apparatus 'for grappling and raising sunken vessels and other submerged bodies' in 1852.

Charles Barnard, the inventor of a machine for making wire netting, was an ironmonger near the market place from around 1826, but moved to Pottergate in 1840, where his firm manufactured agricultural and domestic ironwork. He was the son of a farmer, so he knew there was a huge demand for fencing to keep out foxes and rabbits. In 1844 he invented a wire netting machine, based on a weaving loom. It operated manually, with a man doing the weaving and a boy turning it. He also exhibited galvanised wire netting at the Great Exhibition at the Crystal Palace in 1851, and he patented a self-rolling mangle.

Barnard, Bishop and Barnard (as the firm became known) expanded and became well known for their gates. Thomas Jekyll designed the Norwich Gates, which won a gold medal at the London Exhibition of 1862. A public subscription bought them as a wedding present for Prince of Wales, and they were installed in the royal park at Sandringham in 1864.

The firm also developed something unusual in 1960 – an iron lighthouse for the Brazilian government. The lighthouse was made in sections and had 144 iron plates; it was 17ft in diameter, 46ft tall, and the lantern was 16ft high. It was temporarily put up by the riverside next to St George's Bridge before it was sent to Brazil, and provided quite a spectacle!

However, the most famous invention is by a man that many people don't even realise came from Norwich – Peter Barlow.

Barlow was born in the parish of St Simon on 15 October 1776. He was educated at a local foundation school before becoming a schoolmaster, firstly at an academy in Essex and then in Shipdham. He taught himself algebra, geometry, trigonometry, navigation and French – and the navigation was particularly important in his scientific work in the 1820s.

He contributed articles to the *Ladies Diary*, which was edited by Dr Hutton, the professor of mathematics at the Royal Military Academy at Woolwich.

Peter Barlow. *(Photograph by kind permission of Norwich Castle Museum and Art Gallery)*

Hutton advised Barlow to apply for the post of assistant mathematics master there in 1801. He was successful and while there met Mr Bonnycastle – who was, according to the *Norfolk Chronicle*, 'the means of reducing Mr Barlow's attainments to some systematic order' as apparently his studies hadn't been particularly logical.

In 1814 he published *New Mathematical Tables,* which became known as *Barlow's Tables*. This work gives the factors, squares, cubes, square roots, reciprocals and hyperbolic logarithms of all the numbers from 1 to 10,000. The tables were regularly reprinted and used for many years until they were eventually made obsolete by computers.

He also invented the Barlow Lens, which was an achromatic lens to reduce lens aberration in telescopes. It was made by putting the colourless liquid disulphide of carbon between two pieces of glass. He worked with George Dollond to make the lens out of flint and crown glass and used it on a telescope; it was used by the astronomer William Dawes to measure minute double stars, and Dollond presented the lens to the Royal Society in 1834.

Barlow was awarded the gold medal of the Society of Arts in 1821. He became a fellow of the Royal Society in 1823 and received the Copley Medal (an award which was also given later to Einstein, Darwin and Faraday) in 1825 for his work on magnetism. At the time, many ships were made of iron, and this affected their compasses; Barlow found a solution by fixing a small piece of iron next to the compass to correct the deviation. The Board of Longitude awarded him a grant of £500 for his work and, when the device was used by the Russian Navy in 1824, Tsar Alexander gave him a gold watch and chain.

Barlow also worked with Thomas Telford on the bridge over the Menai Strait, and when Westminster Bridge was replaced in the 1820s, it was only after Barlow had made a report on how the tides on the Thames would be affected by the removal of the old bridge.

In 1847, at the age of 71, he resigned from the Woolwich Academy; however, because of his public services they continued to pay him.

He died at Charlton in Kent on 1 March 1862. The *Norfolk Chronicle's* obituary praised him highly: 'his urbanity of manner and cheerfulness of disposition made him a most delightful companion to both old and young'.

THIRTY-FIVE

The Reformers of Norwich

We've been very lucky with some of our politicians in Norwich – particularly with councillors who were driven to fight for the rights of the less able in society. Here I've included some of the people whose work was so important: Ernest Blyth, who gave children a better life; Mabel Clarkson, a pioneer of women's rights; John Dowson, who taught children for free at a time when education wasn't free; Ruth Hardy, the first 'housewife mayor' of Norwich; Dorothy Jewson, the city's first female MP; and Frederick Jex, who made sure all the children in the city had the chance of a full secondary education.

Ernest Blyth

Ernest Egbert Blyth, LLD, was born at St Faith's Terrace in the parish of St Peter Parmentergate in 1857, the son of timber merchant William Blyth. He was educated at Amersham and took his legal degree in London, winning several Law Society prizes on the way – including the Scott Scholarship for the first year in common law, the Broderip medal for the first year in conveyancing, and the Clifford's Inn prize for being first in the examination as whole. He qualified as a solicitor in 1878, becoming a magistrate as well in 1914.

Blyth made his name in the case of the failure of the Harvey and Hudson Bank and obtained an action against the solicitor Isaac Bugg Coaks, alleging fraud and misappropriation of money. As soon as the case opened in court the defendant consented to judgement (and was subsequently struck off). Most of the time, Blyth's work was in family and conveyancing law. He also founded the Norfolk and Norwich Incorporated Law Society. However, his real impact on the city was

Dr E.E. Blyth. *(Photograph by kind permission of Barrett & Coe)*

in his civic work. In 1910 he was the last Mayor and the first Lord Mayor of Norwich, and he believed in education for all. He was a member of the Norwich School Board of Guardians from 1887 and Norwich Education Committee from 1904 (chairing it from 1916 to 1933 – the *Eastern Daily Press* said 'no more competent chairman could have been chosen'), and he was either a governor or the chair of governors at six Norwich schools.

He was also heavily involved in the Silver Road Mission, helping to give children a better life. One of his kindnesses included giving Christmas presents to the children of the Silver Road Sunday School, who were among the poorest in the city. He gave the Blyth School the Alice Margaret Blyth Memorial Library in honour of his first wife, Alice, and the *Eastern Daily Press* said it was 'considered to be perhaps the best library of any school in the country'.

He was full of energy and, in the 55 years of his working life, he only took 10 days off sick. He was taken ill in his office in Upper King Street on 24 March 1937 and died on 20 April at his home from pneumonia, aged 77. In a tribute to him the day after his death, the *Eastern Daily Press* said, 'So often he would be seen hurrying to fulfil his many professional and public engagements. Few men led a busier life.' They added that he 'seemed reserved', but once you spoke to him you discovered 'a man of great charm and kindliness'.

Ernest Blyth's grave at the Rosary Cemetery. *(Photograph by author)*

Mabel Clarkson

Mabel Maria Clarkson was born on 1 June 1875 in Calne, Wiltshire, the daughter of a solicitor. She was educated in Reading but settled in Norwich, and in 1906 was elected a member of the Norwich Board of Guardians for Ber Street ward. In 1911 she joined Norwich's distress committee, where she took a particular interest in the problems of unemployed women, who were often neglected in relief programmes. She campaigned to get rid of the slums and started workshops in cookery, laundry and sewing for unemployed women to help them earn a living.

In 1913 she was elected as the Liberal councillor for the Town Close ward of Norwich borough council: she was the first woman who had been elected to the council chamber. Her campaign slogan was 'the best wealth of a city is in the health of its citizens', and she spoke out about infant mortality and public health due to overcrowding. She also chaired the city's public assistance committee (which became the social welfare committee), and the *Eastern Daily Press* noted that she wasn't a frequent speaker in debates, 'but when she did speak she had something worthwhile to say' and was always very good on the details.

In 1922 Clarkson became a magistrate. She joined the Labour party and was elected in 1926 for Heigham ward and was also elected as sheriff in 1928 – the first woman and the first member of the Labour Party to be elected to this position. Two years later she became lord mayor of Norwich, the second woman to hold the office (Ethel Colman being the first, in 1923). The *Eastern Daily Press* reported in October 1830:

> For many years she has been in the forefront of the movement for social progress in Norwich. In her administrative work she has been tireless in her application and zealous in her care to sift every jot and tittle [sic] of evidence.

They added that when she was the sheriff, the city appreciated her 'transparent sincerity and honesty of purpose'. During her year as lord mayor, she continued her full work in the council chamber, basically doing two jobs at once.

In 1931 Clarkson was made CBE, and the following year she became a magistrate, a post in which she continued until 1948 when she retired due to ill health. She was a member of the Norwich District Nursing Association and the League of Nations Union, as well as being a leading member of the National Council of Women. She was also the chair of the Norwich Schoolchildren's Boot

Fund from 1921 to 1946, which raised thousands of pounds to provide 'necessitous children with adequate footwear'.

She died on 20 March 1950 at her home in Mount Pleasant, Norwich. The tribute in the *Eastern Evening News* said, 'The public life of Norwich was the poorer when Mabel Clarkson left it. It is not given to many women, or men for that matter, to achieve such an enduring place in the history of their city.'

John Dowson

John Withers Dowson was born on 28 February 1800, the eldest son of a merchant at Geldeston. He was educated at Norwich Grammar School and was articled to solicitors in London. He later returned to Norwich, married and settled down, firstly in Castle Street and then in Prince of Wales Road.

Although he trained in the law, his aptitude was for teaching and he did much for education in the city. Despite having no children of his own, he wanted to help children learn. He held free classes for working-class children in his summer house

John Dowson. *(Photograph by kind permission of Norwich Castle Museum and Art Gallery)*

before and after work. Together with James Martineau, he started a free school at the Octagon Chapel in Colegate. As part of his work there, he organised Sunday school outings and set up a friendly society for the parents of the children he taught, to help if they were sick or unemployed. Eventually he became the superintendent of the Sunday schools in Norwich.

He was a true Victorian philanthropist; he was a founder of the Mechanics Institute in 1823 (where he established a debating class to give people practice in public speaking), a member of the Board of Guardians and a trustee of the Coal and Soup Society.

In 1849 he was one of the three speakers at an evening event celebrating the opening of the People's College in the city. One lecturer gave a phrenological analysis of the heads of the speakers and said that Dowson's head 'showed beautiful Christian developments'.

He died on 12 July 1879 and was buried in the Rosary cemetery. Eulogies at his funeral included a description of his 'clear head, methodical habits...thoughtful and large-hearted kindness'. Others said that he was plain of speech and dress, direct in his approaches, straightforward and open as the day, and showed perfect courtesy. Speakers noted he was a strict teetotaller with simple tastes and unfailing charity: 'Was there sickness or need in some neglected court or alley, Mr Dowson's presence was there, before it was sent for.' However, he was also good company and 'preserved untainted the capacity of a well-nigh boyish enjoyment'. He wasn't a yes-man, either, because he 'would religiously take his own line when he thought it the right line, let who might be against it'.

Ruth Hardy

Ruth Elsie Hardy was born in Lakenheath in 1890, one of 10 children. She was educated at the Norwich Municipal Secondary School (which later merged with the Blyth School) and was known as the 'first housewife Lord Mayor of Norwich' – though, as with many of our best politicians, she was much more than that. She lived in Norwich from 1905 and became a teacher at the Crome School before marrying the senior French master of Eaton CNS.

During World War Two, in November 1941 she created the Magna Old Age Pensioners' clubs – 'Magna' stood for 'Mutual Air Good Neighbours Association'. It was organised in a similar way to the air-raid wardens, covering 1,500 streets and roads with all associated courts. One organiser in each street would act as a 'Street Mother', listing all the elderly people and those more likely to need help after an air raid, and over 30,000 women in Norwich became members, putting a yellow poster in their window that said 'A good neighbour lives here'.

Hardy was also a governor of three schools and the Norwich Consolidated Charities. She became a Labour councillor in 1945, and when she was elected as lord mayor in 1950, she was the third woman to hold the office and the first married woman to do so. Her only child, Marion (a language teacher in Cambridge at the time), acted as her mayoress.

During her civic career Hardy served on the education, library and museum committees, and she was chair of the health committee. She became a magistrate and alderman in 1960, retiring in 1970. In later years she lived in Foulger's

House flats for the elderly and was visited by the Queen Mother when she opened the flats.

She died on 9 February 1975, aged 85, after falling ill the previous week.

Dorothy Jewson

Dorothy Jewson was born in Norwich on 17 August 1884, the daughter of a wealthy coal merchant. She was educated at Cheltenham College and Girton College, Cambridge, where she was involved with the Fabian Society. She taught at Richmond School from 1908 to 1911 and then returned to Norwich to teach at a board school.

Jewson investigated poverty and poor relief in the city and in 1912 published a report written with her brother, entitled *The Destitute of Norwich*. She became a member of the Independent Labour Party, though was unsuccessful when she stood as a Labour candidate for the Board of Guardians in 1912. She was also involved with the Women's Social and Political Union; as a pacifist, she was against Britain's involvement in World War One but helped to run a training school for unemployed girls under the age of 17.

In 1916 she became an organiser for the National Federation of Women's Workers, and in 1923 she was elected as the Labour MP for Norwich – making her one of the first female MPs in the country. *The Times,* when talking about the candidates, mentioned that Jewson 'has been engaged for years in helping to improve the lot of casually employed and badly paid girls and women'.

Jewson had a great deal of integrity and acted according to her beliefs. For example, in December 1923 there was a national rail strike, and she needed to return from London to Norwich. So she walked back with the friend who accompanied her to meetings, Miss Murray. 'In consequence of our sympathy with the men on strike, we did not feel justified in riding on a train,' she said on her return to Norwich. Despite the fact the route meant they would be travelling almost twice as far as they needed to, they went via Bury St Edmunds; firstly, because Jewson wanted to visit the town, and secondly, because she felt it would be better to walk on the quieter roads. They were offered lifts on the way and took them – one on a brick lorry and one on a furniture van, where Jewson said they had to sit on a pile of old books; when they reached Bury, they learned that the strike was over and took a train the rest of the way.

The local newspaper reported that she wasn't at all a proud woman. She lived in a small flat in St Pancras, sharing with a friend, and insisted on doing her share of the housework, including making breakfast. Her friend said to her, 'Won't you stay in bed and rest? You've got a hard day.' Jewson's reaction was immediate: 'No, I'll do it.' The newspaper reported that it was typical of her to do her share: 'That is Dorothy Jewson.'

She lost her seat in 1924 and formed the Workers' Birth Control Group with Dora Russell – a brave move considering that at the time she was still single. The aim was to persuade the government to give free advice on birth control: she thought that this, along with family allowances, was important on grounds of class as well as feminism. However, Ramsey MacDonald argued against it, and the proposal was defeated.

In 1925 she was a member of the committee of inquiry into legal advice for poor prisoners, whose brief was to look into what advice poor prisoners received about their legal rights and liabilities, the aid available in the conduct of legal proceedings and what further steps should be taken.

From 1927 to 1936 Jewson was a member of the city council. She stood as a candidate for parliament twice more, in 1929 and 1931, but was unsuccessful. She continued to be active in the Independent Labour Party and edited their monthly bulletin. She married the tea-merchant Richard Tanner Smith in 1936 and, after he died, she married the Labour MP Campbell Stephen in 1945. During World War Two she became closer to the Society of Friends and became a formal member of the society in 1958.

In 1963 Jewson returned to Norwich and lived in a cottage in the grounds of her brother's house at Hellesdon. She died on 29 February 1964 and was cremated in St Faith's Crematorium.

Frederick Jex

Frederick Jex was born in Norwich on 4 November 1886, the sixth of 12 children. Although he won a scholarship from a board school to a higher grade school, he had to leave school at the age of 14 because his parents couldn't afford to keep him at school. He became an apprentice in the shoe trade, and he was a specialist in turnshoes by 1914, earning up to £2 a week. He became the secretary of the Norwich branch of the National Union of Boot and Shoe Operatives in 1914 and was elected to the National Executive in 1926 and the International Executive in 1934. His aim was to maintain freedom of disputes and to help workers and the industry over their difficulties.

Jex also played a huge part in Norwich's civic life. In 1913, at the age of 27, he became a member of the Board of Guardians. He was described as a 'very slim, pale young man, burning with indignation at the hardships people at that time suffered'. In 1919 he was elected to the city council and won every election until he became an alderman and Justice of the Peace in 1928. He was the chair of the Licensing Justices, and was the Leader of Council from 1931 to 1955. He was also the chair of the Education Committee from 1933 until he stepped down in 1963, and it was said that 83 per cent of children in Norwich were being educated at a school which had been built or improved during his term of office.

Frederick Jex. *(Picture courtesy of Norfolk County Council Library and Information Service)*

Jex campaigned for better schools, decent working conditions and houses with electricity and hot water. He had the chance to become lord mayor in 1930, but refused because of the difficulties in his industry and his view that the workers needed him more. However, he did become lord mayor in 1933 and was later described as one of the most eloquent and forceful lord mayors in living memory. The *Eastern Daily Press* described him as 'one of the ablest and most fluent speakers in the city. A man of sound judgement and fearless expression', and added that he was also very well liked.

Jex was invited to be the candidate for parliament for Norwich but declined; the local papers reported that 'it was known that Mr Jex's wholehearted interest in the public and the administrative life of Norwich appealed to him more strongly than the prospect of fighting for Parliamentary honours'.

During World War Two he was the vice chair of the Norwich war charities. He also loved football and became a director of Norwich City Football Club in 1937 and remained as a director for eight years. In 1946 he was awarded an OBE for his public work, including notable service with the Civil Defence during World War Two.

Lord Mayor Ruth Hardy gave him the Freedom of the City in March 1951 and described him as 'an intensely practical man in his grasp of the details of any immediate problem but, none the less, a man of wide vision and understanding'. At the ceremony there was an audience of 800 in St Andrew's Hall (including '200 senior scholars from every school under the administration of the local Education

Committee'). He was presented with the honorary freeman's parchment scroll in a silver-gilt, ivory-ornamented casket, and Ruth Hardy pointed out that since 1835 only 16 people had been awarded the Freedom of the City.

Hardy added that Jex was gifted, as he had both vision and practicality. She also mentioned that much of his work had been during difficult times, and:

> ...during such a period the affairs of a city can very easily fall into confusion and muddle in the hands either of idealists, who ignore the practical difficulty of the immediate problem, or of those practical people who lack the vision and the sustained purpose necessary for surmounting such immediate difficulties.

In his years on the Education Committee, he worked to reorganise the system so that all Norwich children could have a full secondary education, something that was denied to him. Ruth Hardy added that he had done it 'under the constant handicap of recurring ill-health, sustained by a great will and devotion, never to the purposes of his own advantage but to the welfare of his city and its people'.

Jex himself was far more modest. He said that he was sensible enough to know he was just an ordinary man and certainly not an outstanding person. In his view, the changes had happened because the social conscience of the people had stirred itself sufficiently to make the changes. One of the things that had really upset him was 40 years before, when he saw unemployed skilled craftsmen in the shoe trade who had to appeal to the Guardians and 'were herded together to do wood chopping in Museum Court'. This inspired him to make changes so it wouldn't happen again.

Jex died in 1968. The *Eastern Daily Press* said in his obituary that his years of public service were 'characterised by his high sense of responsibility and an anxiety to put the welfare of the city above party differences'. He definitely succeeded, because Sir Robert Bignold, his political opponent, said, 'I found him to be a bitter opponent sometimes, but always ready to hear the other point of view and I had complete trust in Mr Jex.' In addition Cecil Sutton, the leader of the city council, summed him up perfectly:

> He was a man who, if he had not decided to stop in the city of his birth, could have risen to far greater heights in national politics...a man who was held in the highest regard by all members of the council.